978.953 W373o

Weber, David J.

On the edge of empire

DATE DUE

DEMCO 38-297

ENTERED MAY 27 1997

On the Edge of Empire:

The Taos Hacienda of los Martínez

On the Edge of Empire:

The Taos Hacienda

of Los Martínez

By David J. Weber

With a Photographic Essay by Anthony Richardson
Narrative text by Skip Miller

Museum of New Mexico Press   Santa Fe

Published in Cooperation with
the William P. Clements Center for Southwest Studies,
Southern Methodist University, and SMU-in-Taos, Fort Burgwin

Photographer's Dedication
To
John Francis Fairbanks and the
men of the USS *Edsel*
and
John T. Gordon

```
978.953 W373o

Weber, David J.

On the edge of empire
```

Copyright © 1996 Museum of New Mexico Press. *All rights reserved.* No part of this book may be reproduced in any form or by any means whatsoever without the expressed written consent of the publisher, with the exception of brief passages embodied in critical reviews.

Kit Carson Historic Museums wishes to thank Kodak for their generous grant of materials for the photographic essay portion of this book.

Project Editor: Mary Wachs
Copy Editor: Denice Anderson
Design: Susan Surprise
Maps: Deborah Reade
Composition: Set in Garamond with Albertus and Lucida Blackletter display type.

Manufactured in the United States of America
10 9 8 7 6 5 4 3 2 1

Library of Congress Cataloging-in-Publication Data
Weber, David J.
    On the edge of empire: the Taos hacienda of los Martínez/David J. Weber; with photo essay text by Skip Miller.
       p.   cm.
    Includes bibliographical references and index.
    ISBN 0–89013–299–2 (cloth).—ISBN 0–89013–301–8 (pbk.)
    1. Severino Martinez House (Taos, N.M.) 2. Martinez, Antonio Severino, 1761–1827. 3. Haciendas—New Mexico—Taos—History. 4. Martínez family. 5. Taos (N.M.)—History.   I. Title.
F804. T2W4 1996
978.9'53—dc20
                                                     96–10173
                                                       CIP

Contents

INTRODUCTION	1
1. Pioneers on the Chama	5
Pioneers. Abiquiú. Peace and Expansion.	
2. A Landed Estate in Taos	17
Taos. Land and Labor.	
3. Markets, Mules, and Prosperity	33
Markets. The *Alcalde* and the Mule. Affluence.	
4. Twilight of Empire	42
"Barbaric" Indians and Anglo Americans. A Priest in the Family.	
5. Winds of Change: A Mexican Territory	48
Don Severino in Territorial Politics. The Parish Priest.	
6. Don Severino and the North Americans	57
Taos and the Santa Fe Trail. The *Alcalde* and the *Extranjeros*. The Robidoux-Vigil Imbroglio. Mexicans and Americans.	
7. The Patriarch's Legacy	69
Last Will and Testament. Sons of the Patriarch. The Martínez Brothers and the American Takeover.	
A Photographic Tour	
La Hacienda de los Martínez.	
8. The Casa Mayor	83
The New Mexico Manor House. The House Divided. The House Preserved.	
Appendix	97
"The Last Will and Testament of Don Severino Martínez [1827]."	
Acknowledgments	111
Abbreviations Used in the Notes	113
For Further Reading	115
Index	117

❖

These houses had been built as forts. With walls three or four feet thick they enclosed each a courtyard, called a placita, and behind this was always another square enclosed by a high adobe wall with quarters for slaves and peons built inside it. Here the carts and wagons were kept and the horses could be driven in when danger threatened. Windows were barred and a trusted servant asked every comer his name and business before doors were opened. Storerooms were filled with grain and dried buffalo meat and a well in the courtyard supplied water. Life here was secure. It was shut in and well nourished. Each great house reproduced the isolation which beset the colony as a whole.

Harvey Fergusson, *Rio Grande* (1931)

Introduction

For nearly two centuries the sprawling one-story adobe house of Severino and María del Carmel Martínez has occupied a site on the bank of a small stream, the Río del Pueblo, two miles southwest of the Taos plaza in a neighborhood known as Ranchitos de Abajo, or Lower Ranchitos. Abandoned for years and fallen into ruins, the old adobe recently won a new lease on life. It now stands open to the public as the finest remaining example of a Spanish Colonial manor house in the Taos Valley, if not in all of New Mexico, thanks to the initiative and restoration work of the administrators at the Kit Carson Historic Museums.

The Martínez house today consists of twenty-one rooms arranged around two central courtyards, or *placitas*. Constructed from the first with defense in mind, it presents an austere, windowless facade to the outside world. Its residents looked inward. Doors from every room opened onto the courtyards, and, like the close-knit family that made this house a home, many of the rooms connected with one another.

In southwestern America this kind of large Mexican-style house, built around a courtyard or courtyards, has come to be called an "hacienda." South of the border, however, the word "hacienda" suggests more than a manor house. In Mexico, an hacienda has meant a great landed estate, of which the manor house is only a part. So it was originally with the Martínez hacienda, whose founders, Severino and María Martínez, slowly acquired extensive properties around their house—an estate or hacienda that stretched as far as the eye could see. As their hacienda grew and prospered, so too did their house and household.

In its rural mountain valley setting and with its period furnishings, the great house of Severino and María Martínez offers today's visitors remarkable glimpses into the ambience and material world of New Mexico's elite in the early nineteenth century, when the province belonged first to Spain and then to

Mexico. Unfortunately, the day-to-day concerns of that era have disappeared from view. Blacktop covers the dirt road that once led through dust or mud to the hacienda. Tourism has outstripped agriculture and ranching as the economic mainstay of the Taos Valley. Boutiques and galleries have replaced the tradesmen whose shops once lined the Taos plaza. The United States has superseded Spain and Mexico as sovereign, and English has supplanted Spanish as the prevailing language in all of New Mexico.

We cannot recapture in detail the early years of the Martínez hacienda or know what its residents thought or how they looked. In broad outline, though, we can understand much about this remarkable place in time and about the stunning political, economic, cultural, and social changes that the Martínez family experienced there.

Severino Martínez and his wife had grown up in the late eighteenth century on the northern frontier of New Mexico, a province that itself stood at the outer edge of Spain's far-flung New World empire. Like other New Mexicans of their generation, they grew up with the harsh reality of Indian attacks, but by the mid-1780s, as don Severino entered his twenties, New Mexicans came to terms with many of their Apache, Comanche, and Navajo adversaries. New Mexico entered a period of relative peace and prosperity that lasted for more than two decades. In the 1810s, when don Severino had reached his fifties, wars of independence began to tear apart the Spanish Empire, devastating the colonies from Mexico to Argentina. New Mexico's economy suffered during this decade of insurgency, as did its relations with neighboring tribes of independent nomads.

In 1821, don Severino's sixtieth year, Mexico won independence from Spain, ushering in a new era. As residents of newly independent Mexico, New Mexicans joined their countrymen on the journey from monarchy to republicanism, from subject to citizen, from closed markets to free trade, and from an insular Hispanic world to one open to foreigners and foreign ideas—particularly those from the neighboring United States. At this juncture Taos began to receive a remarkable number of visitors and immigrants from the United States. Thus, the roots of Taos's unusual multiethnic heritage go back to the 1820s, to don Severino's last years.

Severino Martínez rode the crest of these waves of change to become one of the most prosperous and powerful Hispanics in the Taos Valley. When he died in 1827, he left an impressive estate for a New Mexican of his day. He enumerated his holdings in an unusually detailed will that still survives. (Ably translated into English by Ward Alan Minge, it appears as an appendix in this volume.) Don Severino also left behind his wife, who died two years after him, and six children. The eldest, Antonio José, may have given his parents the most reason for pride because he became a priest. After his parents' deaths, Padre Martínez (1793–1867) went on to become one of the most striking figures in the nineteenth-century Southwest—perhaps even, in the words of his biographer, New Mexico's "major genius in his own century as well as those before and after his time."[1] Clearly, the son's reputation has eclipsed that of his father. Don Severino's legacy, however, also included a large house, which has survived neglect and the forces of modernity to represent the era in which he lived, a time just before the priest overshadowed the patriarch.

The idea for this book originated with R. C. Gordon-McCutchan in the late summer of 1992. Then serving as acting director of the Kit Carson Historic Museums (which administers the Kit Carson home, the Ernest Blumenschein home, and the Martínez hacienda), R. C. asked me to write an essay that would situate the early years of the Martínez hacienda in time and place. That task proved more difficult than either of us imagined. Notwithstanding the prominence of Padre Martínez in New Mexico history, little was known about his parents, Severino and María, or the house that they built. Similarly, although Taos had enjoyed an international reputation as a center for artists in the twentieth century, the village's early history remained hazily understood. Currents of misinformation and myth run through many of the historical accounts of early Taos.

The problem has been exacerbated by the meagerness of the historical record. Most of the sources for the history of the early years vanished in the so-called Taos Rebellion of 1847, when rebels seized the town's archives and tore up the documents.[2] For good reason, then, a sophisticated, thoroughly documented history of early Taos has yet to be written and may never be.[3] Sources that do remain relate primarily to politics, economics, and the law—public arenas dominated by males that reveal little about the private sphere of women in early New Mexico. In telling the story of the Martínez clan, we know more about the lives of fathers and sons than about mothers and daughters.

Despite the paucity of the public record in Taos itself, I have been fortunate to find some surprising stories in documents that survived in the Spanish and Mexican archives of New Mexico, in the accounts by foreigners who visited New Mexico, and in previously uncited private papers belonging to Pascual Martínez, the youngest son of Severino, who eventually came to own all of the Martínez hacienda. These fragments of information offer rare views of a dynamic era in Spanish and Mexican Taos, when a family patriarch and his wife built an enduring manor house.

Although this story focuses on Severino Martínez and the making of his hacienda in the early nineteenth century, it does not neglect the adobe's decline in the twentieth century and its restoration in the 1980s by the Kit Carson Historic Museums. More powerfully than a narrator's words, however, photographs document the hacienda's modern decline and recent reconstruction. The files of the Kit Carson Historic Museums have yielded some remarkable images from the early twentieth century. Four unpublished photographs by early Taos painter E. Irving Couse are included along with a complete photographic document of the restoration by Anthony Richardson, who donated his time and talent to this project. A room-by-room tour of the restored hacienda by Skip Miller, codirector and curator of the Kit Carson Historic Museums, offers an intimate view of the structure, its furnishings, its exhibits, and its setting. Skip's essay will delight and inform visitors who take the time to stroll through the rooms and courtyards of the picturesque hacienda that Severino and María del Carmel Martínez built by the clear waters of the Río del Pueblo.

The book concludes with the last will and testament of Severino Martínez, drawn up in 1827. Ward Alan Minge brought that document to light when he translated and published it in 1963. Scholars quickly recognized the will's importance, not only for understanding the holdings of don Severino but for yielding remarkable detail about the material culture of northern New Mexico. We have reproduced Dr. Minge's translation of the will in its entirety, a document essential to understanding the early years of the Martínez hacienda yet difficult to find in its earlier imprint.

David J. Weber,
Summer 1994

Notes

1. Angélico Chávez, *But Time and Chance: The Story of Padre Martínez of Taos, 1793–1867* (Santa Fe: Sunstone Press, 1981), 160.

2. J. J. Bowden, "Private Land Claims in the Southwest," 6 vols. (LL.M. [master of laws] thesis, Southern Methodist University, 1969), 4:918. For the period before American occupation, most community records—including those for Taos—have disappeared. Henry Putney Beers, *Spanish & Mexican Records of the American Southwest* (Tucson: University of Arizona Press, 1979), 63–64.

3. The anecdotal work of Blanche C. Grant, *When Old Trails Were New: The Story of Taos* (New York: Press of the Pioneers, 1934), remains the best overview, although aspects of Taos history have been ably explored in a number of books and articles. Even fragmentary records can yield a great deal of information; a more sophisticated history of Taos is long overdue. For a splendid guide to the types of records available for community studies in New Mexico, see John L. Kessell, "Sources for the History of a New Mexico Community: Abiquiú," *NMHR* 54 (October 1979):249–85.

CHAPTER
❖ ONE

Pioneers on the Chama

Severino and María Martínez had long known the harshness of daily life at the outer edges of Hispanic New Mexico. Before moving to the Taos Valley in 1804 they had made their home in the parish of Abiquiú at the Plaza de Santa Rosa de la Capilla—Saint Rose of the Little Chapel. Some forty-five miles northwest of New Mexico's capital, Santa Fe, this was one of several isolated farming villages, known to their residents as *puestos* or *plazas*, in the Chama River valley.[1]

Pioneers

Both Severino and María del Carmel came from families with long pioneering traditions. Like numerous Martíns and Martínezes in northern New Mexico, Severino's antecedents may trace back to two brothers from Zacatecas, Mexico, Hernán and Luis Martín Serrano, who ventured into New Mexico with don Juan de Oñate in 1598 and helped establish a permanent Spanish presence amid the Pueblo Indians on the Río Grande.[2] Subsequent generations continued that frontier tradition. In the 1730s, Severino's grandparents probably helped to establish the Plaza of Santa Rosa de Lima de Abiquiú, on the edge of the Ute territory.[3] In midcentury, residents abandoned the village briefly in the face of Ute and Comanche raids. When they returned, the residents built a new plaza about a mile downstream, calling it the Plaza de Santa Rosa de la Capilla or the Plaza de la Capilla.[4]

There the little community survived but did not flourish. Its population remained small and its chapel humble. A Franciscan who inspected the chapel in 1776 found it decorated by nothing more than "a paper print" of Saint Rose of Lima with a "set of vestments so old that even to look at it is indecorous."[5]

The Plaza de Santa Rosa de la Capilla stood on the south bank of the Chama River about a mile and a half east of present Abiquiú, a Hispanicized Indian (*genízaro*) town founded in the 1750s. Today, nearly all traces of the Santa Rosa de la Capilla have vanished, carried away by a shift in the river. Only the stabilized ruins of its chapel remain visible.[6]

In the chapel of Santa Rosa, or in the nearby church of Santo Tomás in Abiquiú, Severino was apparently baptized on January 13, 1761, one of at least three children of José Martín and Micaela Valdés.[7] Although his baptismal name was Antonio, he went by Severino—perhaps to avoid confusion with his older brother, Antonio José.[8] His parents were apparently *mestizos*—persons of mixed Spanish and Indian blood. In racially conscious New Mexico society, however, they had acquired sufficient status to be regarded as Spaniards, or *españoles*, in some records; or, as the priest noted more obliquely in the baptismal register, they could be regarded as Spaniards—"*tenidos por españoles*"—a common expression in New Mexico.[9] Little is known of Antonio Severino's parents except that late in life his father, José, served as a magistrate at the Plaza de Santa Rosa de la Capilla as early as 1779 and as late as 1804.[10]

Through much of his life Severino used his father's surname, Martín, interchangeably with Martínez. His neighbors knew him by both names, although late in life he preferred to sign his name "Martínes" or "Martínez."[11] The reason for the name change remains obscure, but one authority suggests that the large family came to be known as the Martíns—"los Martínes"—and the substitution of a final "z" for the final "s" eventually turned this plural form into "Martínez."[12] Among his contemporaries, don Severino was not alone in using Martín and Martínez interchangeably.[13]

María del Carmel also descended from several generations of Hispanic frontiersmen.[14] Her father's side of the family, the Santistebans (also spelled

Santistevan or Santiestevan), claimed descent from Spanish Creoles who settled in New Mexico shortly after Diego de Vargas reconquered the province from Pueblo rebels in 1693. María del Carmel's grandparents may have come from Santa Cruz de la Cañada, and her parents, Juan Antonio Santisteban Coronel and Francisca de la Luz Trujillo, were among the founders of the village of La Cañada de Cochití.[15] At least three of their children were born in that isolated plaza, but María del Carmel was probably born about 1773 in the neighborhood of Abiquiú, where her family seems to have moved to in the early 1770s.[16]

During María del Carmel's childhood and Antonio Severino's teenage years, New Mexicans endured a protracted crisis, one that began in the 1750s and reached its apogee in the 1770s. Comanche, Gileño Apache, and Navajo raiders devastated the province, killing Hispanos and Pueblo Indians, stealing horses and other livestock, paralyzing agriculture, and forcing the abandonment of many small towns. Abiquiú residents tried to abandon the town in 1770 and 1771, but Gov. Pedro Fermín de Mendinueta refused to let them leave.[17] Antonio Severino and María del Carmel survived those bitter years, when many New Mexicans suffered from drought and hunger. They also lived through the great smallpox epidemic of 1780–81, which killed 20 to 25 percent of their neighbors.[18]

On March 25, 1787, when he was twenty-six years old and she about fourteen, Antonio Severino and María del Carmel married at Abiquiú—perhaps in the chapel of Santa Rosa.[19] Following local custom, he most likely wore his hair in two long braids that hung down his shoulders; she probably braided her hair in a knot, piled atop her head, and gave her cheeks a crimson blush with the crushed flowers from a plant called *alegría*.[20]

Severino brought to their marriage thirteen head of cattle, a horse, a saddle "in fair condition," 175 *varas* of land of his own, and a third interest in one hundred more varas of land that he owned with his two brothers. María del Carmel apparently had little to contribute to the marital assets.[21] When her parents died, she inherited only twenty varas of land, which she later sold for a bull.[22]

In arid New Mexico, Hispanos measured irrigable land by a unit of length—the vara, equivalent to thirty-three inches or a single step. They had no need to measure the entire area of their farming lands. Instead, they only calculated the frontage of streams and rivers with the understanding that their property extended back from those watercourses to the edge of the valley floor where the relatively flat, irrigable land ended in foothills or at cliffs.[23]

Severino and María made their first home at the Plaza de Santa Rosa de la Capilla in the parish of Abiquiú. There they lived in a world of kinfolk. At the nearby Plaza de San Miguel, for example, María del Carmel's sister and Antonio Severino's brother also lived together as man and wife.[24]

Abiquiú

Popular writers have often described Abiquiú in breathless prose. "Abiquiú is to New Mexico what Salem is to Massachusetts," claimed one amateur historian whose imagination outstripped his evidence: "A witch lurked behind every adobe wall, and a wizard was doling out love potions that kept husbands home at night."[25] Many New Mexicans did believe in supernatural forces, those sanctioned by the Catholic church as well as some that the church condemned or overlooked,[26] but there is no reason to suppose that Abiquiú had more than its share of witches. In fact, the particulars of everyday life in eighteenth-century Abiquiú, as with other New Mexico villages, went largely unrecorded. The spirit of the era, however, has remained alive in oral tradition. Hispanos living along the Chama River today recall the distant past as a time of scarcity, isolation, tension with neighboring tribes, and hard but satisfying work. They know, in the words of two anthropologists, that "they are descended from a poor people . . . who made their own livings and their own destinies."[27]

Poor the villagers may have been by the reckoning of their descendants, and Severino and María del Carmel may have worn buckskins and lived in adobes of spartan simplicity, but their property and family background gave them high status in the community. Later in Taos, and perhaps when they lived at Abiquiú as well, their neighbors knew them by the honorific title of "don" and "doña"; years later, their oldest son would describe his parents as "Mexicanos" of the "noble" class.[28] Outside of Santa Fe, only 15 percent of Hispano men in New Mexico were literate, and don Severino could count himself among that select group.[29] In 1797, he and one Juan Martín, apparently a relative, together wrote to the governor "in the name of the other residents" of Santa Rosa de la Capilla in a case involving a dispute over water with their *genízaro* neighbors in Abiquiú.[30] Relatives who were probably less educated than don Severino relied upon him to oversee distributions from a will in 1804.[31]

Severino Martínez valued formal education for his male children. His oldest child, Antonio José, recalled that he began primary school in Abiquiú in October 1797 at age five, learning within two years "to read correctly, write, and do some arithmetic."[32] Little is known of schools in eighteenth-century New Mexico; his parents may have sent him to an informal school taught by a priest or a neighbor.[33] Antonio José's sisters and mother, conversely, probably did not know how to read or write. In their rural and patriarchal society, women had little need or encouragement to acquire those skills. They did, though, acquire domestic skills from older women who showed them how to prepare food, treat illness, care for children, manage a household, and recount family traditions through stories that lived on from one generation to the next.[34]

If the Martínez family followed the example of their neighbors on the Chama River, they made their livelihood from farming, herding, hunting, and trading. On lands granted by the Crown, they raised sheep and other stock. In the narrow bottomlands of the Chama they grew corn, wheat, and other crops, including *punche*, a kind of tobacco, raised illegally since the Crown regulated and taxed the sale of tobacco. Living amid hostile Indians, they farmed at some peril; in time of great danger from Indians they retreated to their fortified village and a house with a tower, or *torreón*—a defensive feature often found in remote New Mexican villages. They also bartered with potentially hostile Indian neighbors, such as the Utes, who came to Abiquiú every autumn to trade.[35]

In defiance of government strictures, the Martínez clan may have traveled into the mountainous country to the northwest, in present Colorado, to trade in the country of the Utes.[36] Some traders from the Abiquiú area ventured as far as the Great Basin, exchanging corn, wheat, flour, tobacco, and horses for dressed deer hides, buffalo robes, chamois, and captive Indians whom they "ransomed."[37] If children, these captive Indians were often raised as servants in the households of the *nuevomexicanos;* if adults, they might be sold illegally in Chihuahua, and other points south. In either case, the ransomed Indians lost contact with their tribes and their cultures and became Hispanicized. Hispanics in New Mexico knew these detribalized Indians and their immediate descendants as a separate class of people whom they called *genízaros*.[38] By 1750, *genízaros* constituted 10 percent of the population of Hispanic New Mexico; by the late eighteenth century, the percentage had risen to one-third.[39] Only with the passage of generations did *genízaros* merge into the general Hispanic population.

Severino Martínez grew up just downstream from the pueblo of Santo Tomás de Abiquiú, where in 1754 Gov. Tomás Vélez Cachupín had authorized New Mexico's only mission for *genízaros*.[40] Like his contemporaries, Severino Martínez probably regarded the residents of the Indian town as inferior—persons who lacked the status of *vecino*, or Spanish resident.[41] As a teenager, Severino had at least one *genízara* servant in his household—a Comanche girl ten years younger than he.[42] His parents also reared a part-Indian child, María Gertrudis Martín, who might have been his half sister. The parish priest recorded that the child, whom he baptized on June 3, 1779, was the illegitimate daughter of Severino's father, José. Years later, in his will, Severino described María Gertrudis as his former servant. She had accompanied the family to Taos, where she married.⁴³

Peace and expansion

Severino and María married at a time when New Mexico had begun to see extraordinary growth in population and production. Following the devastating smallpox epidemic of 1780–81, the *vecino* population of New Mexico surged. From some eighty-eight hundred in 1779, New Mexico's Hispanic population rose to twenty-four thousand by 1800 and reached nearly forty thousand by 1820.⁴⁴ At the same time, per capita production rose steadily from the mid-1780s to 1815, beginning a period of unprecedented prosperity for Hispanic New Mexico's modest barter economy.⁴⁵

Several new circumstances had combined to change the economic trajectory of the remote and impoverished province. First, the mid-1780s began a long period of peace between Hispanic New Mexicans, Pueblo Indians, and the native peoples who surrounded them—primarily Comanches, Navajos, and Apaches. Negotiations carried out in the mid-1780s by an exceptionally able governor, Juan Bautista de Anza, led to a Comanche-Spanish alliance in 1786 that became the cornerstone for building peace treaties with other tribes. For the next quarter century, Indians and Hispanics alike lowered the level of violence toward one another.⁴⁶

Second, the Hispanics' former enemies now became their customers for sheep, grain, and textiles. Instead of raiding New Mexican settlements to obtain those goods, Indians received them through government largess. Beginning in 1787 (the year that Severino and María married), New Mexican officials could draw on a special fund sent north from more prosperous areas of New Spain to buy peace on the frontier. With that fund, New Mexican officials purchased livestock, food, clothing, tools, and other articles to give to Indian allies in order to maintain their loyalty and preserve peace. The infusion of outside funds to buy goods to pay off potential Indian raiders had important side effects for New Mexicans, stimulating all sectors of the local economy and providing hard cash to a province that had suffered a dearth of specie.⁴⁷ In 1803 Gov. Fernando de Chacón could report on "excessive display of luxuries" in New Mexico in comparison to other provinces in northern New Spain. "One sees [here] no nakedness or begging."⁴⁸

Third, New Mexicans enjoyed a growing demand for their grain, livestock, hides, and textiles in markets to the south. New silver mines opened up near Chihuahua, Parral, Guanajuato, and Durango in the 1760s and 1770s, and major reforms introduced by Spain under the reign of Charles III (1759–1788) stimulated commerce in general.[49]

Finally, the rising demand for their products and peace with their Indian neighbors encouraged Hispanics to expand production by establishing ranches and farms in new lands once considered highly dangerous.[50] At the same time, it seems likely that older fields and pastures had been depleted by years of intensive farming and grazing and that the growing population crowded the older walled villages, pushing *vecinos* toward new frontiers.[51]

It may have been such pushes and pulls that encouraged Severino and María del Carmel Martínez to leave the Chama Valley. Clearly the villages around the Plaza de Santa Rosa de la Capilla saw rapid growth at this time, due in part to the absorption of many *genízaros* into the *vecino* population. In 1776, one Franciscan put the population of Santa Rosa de Lima at forty-nine families—254 persons;[52] about 1790, a generation later, census takers found eight plazas in the vicinity, with a total of 209 families (not counting the *genízaro* town of Santo Tomás).[53]

Crowded at home and attracted by opportunities to acquire more land, many residents of the little plazas on the Chama moved on to new frontiers,[54] much as Anglo Americans surged across the Appalachians in the years before the War of 1812. In 1804, Severino and María Martínez joined this mobile generation of Hispanic pioneers. They took their three young children and moved into the Taos Valley, a place no less remote than the Chama, where relatives apparently had settled before them.[55]

Although they built a new life in Taos, Severino and María never abandoned their interests in the Plaza de Santa Rosa de la Capilla. Until the end of his life, Severino maintained his property there—his tract of 175 varas of land and his third of a one hundred–vara tract. With his two brothers, he also owned the two-room house and *torreón* that had belonged to his parents in the Plaza de la Capilla. In the same plaza, he owned three rooms in another house, and, in the nearby village of Rito Colorado of Abiquiú, he owned still another room and 110 varas of land.[56]

By retaining his ties to Abiquiú, both financial and familial, and by building ties to new communities as his relatives moved beyond Abiquiú, Severino Martínez came to enjoy considerable influence in the Río Arriba—the Hispanic stronghold north of Santa Fe. As historian Howard Roberts Lamar once imagined the family of Severino and his descendants:

❖

The Martinez tribe stretched throughout the Río Arriba, knitted together in a complex web of consanguinity more characteristic of an old paternalistic society than of a frontier one. And in true patron tradition they and their relations controlled scores of devoted peons, domesticated Indians, and retainers. Though there were many feuds and personality conflicts between rival families, they felt a common bond of blood and environment.[57]

Notes

1. An Abiquiú census of 1790 lists Antonio Severino (25 [29?]) and his wife, María Santistevan (17), as living at the "Plaza de Santa Rosa Capia." This census is most easily consulted in Virginia Langham Olmsted, comp., *Spanish and Mexican Censuses of New Mexico, 1750 to 1830* (Albuquerque: New Mexico Genealogical Society, 1981), 117. The original Abiquiú census is in the Bancroft Library, University of California, Berkeley, in the collection called "New Mexico Originals" (a microfilm edition is in the Zimmerman Library at the University of New Mexico). Olmsted read the age of Severino on this census as twenty-five, but the number could be read twenty-nine just as easily since the census taker's fives and nines were quite similar. I suspect the number is twenty-nine rather than twenty-five, since Severino's birthdate appears to be in January 1761. John Kessell kindly furnished me with a photocopy of that page of the original census.

Severino's will identifies the "pueblo" of Santo Tomás de Abiquiú as the place where he was raised, married, and lived until moving to Taos in 1804. Ward Alan Minge, ed. and trans., "The Last Will and Testament of Don Severino Martínez," *New Mexico Quarterly* 33 (Spring 1963):37. He did not mean literally, however, that he lived within the village of Santo Tomás itself, for it is clear that he lived in the nearby Plaza de Santa Rosa de la Capilla. Since that plaza was in the jurisdiction of the town of Santo Tomás, though, Severino referred to himself as a resident of Santo Tomás. Similarly, in his will of 1827 Severino referred to himself as a resident of "San Geronimo de Taos" (p. 36), referring to the nearby Indian Pueblo of Taos. His will also refers to his residence at the "plaza de San Fernando de San Geronimo de Taos" (p. 40), suggesting that he was identifying San Gerónimo as the jurisdiction of his parish—a word I am using loosely since an Indian mission served by a member of the regular clergy was not, strictly speaking, a parish.

2. New Mexico's leading student of Hispanic families points to this family origin but notes the impossibility of tracing the Martínez clan directly to the first Martín Serrano brothers. Angélico Chávez, *But Time and Chance: The Story of Padre Martínez of Taos, 1793–1867* (Santa Fe: Sunstone Press, 1981), 14–15. Chávez dispels some of the myths surrounding family origins. See, too, Frances León Swadesh, *Los Primeros Pobladores: Hispanic Americans of the Ute Frontier* (Notre Dame: University of Notre Dame Press, 1974), 31–32 (a revised edition, bearing a modified title and name of author, is worth consulting: Francis León Quintana, *Pobladores: Hispanic Americans of the Ute Frontier* [Los Ojos: Ganados del Valle, 1991]). Martín and Martínez may be the most common family name in northern New Mexico. See Roger D. Martínez and J. Michael Gaddis, eds., *Los*

Martines, 1598–1900 (Boulder: Los Martines, 1992), which does not include Severino, his parents, or his children!

3. Severino's father, José, might have been a son of Miguel Martín Serrano and María Archuleta. In his will, dated at Puesto de San Antonio, June 5, 1753, Miguel Martín Serrano refers to his ranch at Abiquiú and to *gamusas* owed him by some Indians, suggesting involvement in the Indian trade (SANM, roll 3, frame 1020). See, too, Fray Angélico Chávez, *Origins of New Mexico Families* (1st ed., 1954; Santa Fe: William Gannon, 1957), 225. The "puesto de San Antonio" where Martín Serrano signed his will also may have been in the Abiquiú area (Swadesh, *Los Primeros Pobladores,* 44). This appears to be the same Miguel Martín Serrano whom Salazar identifies as among the founders of Santa Rosa de Abiquiú. J. Richard Salazar, "Santa Rosa de Lima de Abiquiu," *New Mexico Architecture* 18 (September–October 1976):16–17.

4. The circa 1790 census notes the existence of two plazas named for the chapel of Santa Rosa. One is called the "Plaza de Santa Rosa Capia" and the other the Plaza Santa Rosa de Lima. These two plazas have been described as the single village of Santa Rosa de Lima. See Salazar, "Santa Rosa de Lima," 13–19. Clearly, though, two discrete plazas existed bearing the name of Santa Rosa. Swadesh, *Los Primeros Pobladores,* 38, suggests that Santa Rosa de Lima was later known as La Puente and that it was destroyed by Indians and supplanted by a newer "Plaza de la Capilla," built downstream about a mile. However, the circa 1790 census indicates that the older name (if not the older site) remained in use. Perhaps more research will clarify this; meanwhile, I have followed Swadesh. See, too, Jeffrey L. Boyer, "La Puente: Eighteenth-Century Hispanic Village Life on the Río Chama Frontier," in Bradley J. Vierra and Clara Gualtieri, eds., *Current Research on the Late Prehistory and Early History of New Mexico* (Albuquerque: New Mexico Archaeological Council Special Publication 1, July 1992), 227–38.

5. Eleanor B. Adams and Angélico Chávez, eds. and trans., *Missions of New Mexico, 1776: A Description by Fray Atanasio Domínguez* (Albuquerque: University of New Mexico Press, 1956), 126.

6. I am here following Salazar, "Santa Rosa de Lima de Abiquiu," presuming that Swadesh's Plaza de la Capilla is the same community that Salazar understands to be "Santa Rosa de Lima." Through the confusing changes, the name of the chapel remained consistent—Santa Rosa de Lima—and the possibility exists that the two plazas noted in the 1790 census (Santa Rosa de Lima and Santa Rosa de la Capilla) were not far apart, as Swadesh asserts, but that they were contiguous to the chapel and so appeared as a single community to outsiders. The ruins of the chapel are listed today in the National Register of Historic Places.

7. The couple's known children were Antonio José (1750), Rosa (1759), and Antonio [Severino?] (1761). Chávez, *But Time and Chance,* 15.

8. In his will, for example, he identifies himself by his full name, Antonio Severino, but signs the will "Severino Martínez." For the baptism, see Chávez, *But Time and Chance,* 15, who notes that this son, Antonio, baptized on January 13, 1761, "could very well be . . . Antonio Severino." Although there is no doubt about the names of the parents of Antonio Severino, the identification of their son Antonio, baptized in 1761, cannot be absolutely certain—they may have had still another son, Antonio Severino, for whom we have no baptismal record.

9. Chávez, *But Time and Chance,* 15. For the meaning of that expression, used by other clerics, see Adrian Bustamante, " 'The Matter Was Never Resolved': The Casta System in Colonial New Mexico, 1693–1823," *NMHR* 66 (April 1991):148.

10. Chávez, *But Time and Chance,* 15–16, reports that José held the title of "*teniente*" at those times; his office was probably that of "*teniente de justicia*" or assistant alcalde. Marc Simmons, *Spanish Government in New Mexico* (Albuquerque: University of New Mexico Press, 1968), 161. The parents of Antonio Severino do not appear in the Abiquiú census of 1793. Olmsted, *Spanish and Mexican Censuses,* 111–24.

11. See the petition of Juan and Severino Martín to Gov. Fernando de Chacón, Puesto de Santa Rosa de Abiquiú circa 1797, Gonzales Papers, Ayer Collection, no. 1097A, Newberry Library, Chicago, Illinois, in which Severino signs his name Martínez. See, too, Severino "Martines" to Juan de Dios Peña, Taos, May 5, 1819, in the case of Severino Martín versus Francisco Sánchez, in SANM, roll 19, frames 103–4. In other papers in the case, don Severino's contemporaries refer to him as "Martín," and he

himself signs his name that way (ibid., frames 105–25). The "s" and "z" were used interchangeably and often scribbled in a manner that makes it difficult to distinguish between them. The change from Martín to Martínez began to take place earlier than most writers have assumed. Chávez, *But Time and Chance*, 13, erroneously places the change in the 1820s, attributing it to Padre Martínez, following his return from the seminary.

12. Chávez, *Origins of New Mexico Families*, 226. For Chávez's later speculations on this, see *But Time and Chance*, 13–14.

13. See, for example, Juan Antonio Martines to Gov. Antonio Narbona, Taos, July 20, 1826, and Juan Antonio Martín to the governor [Taos], n.d. [1826], both in MANM, roll 5, frames 540–41 and 1006–7. On one occasion he appears to have written Martín then added an "ez" as an afterthought (Minutes of the Territorial Assembly, July 16, 1825, in MANM, roll 42, frame 277).

14. Because a number of family members, including her husband and son, Antonio José, refer to her as "María del Carmel," I have followed that use. See, for example, [Antonio José Martínez], *Historia cons[c]isa del cura de Taos Antonio José Martínez* (Taos: Vicente F. Romero, 1861); the will of Severino Martínez, and the burial entry for María del Carmel, all cited below. That name is not as common as María del Carmen, by which name she also appears in the work of a number of secondary writers, most notably Angélico Chávez. As an example that Carmen and Carmel were used interchangeably in New Mexico, Sandra Jaramillo Macias, archivist at the State Records Center and Archives in Santa Fe, points to Angélico Chávez, *Archives of the Archdiocese of Santa Fe, 1678–1900* (Washington, D.C.: Academy of Franciscan History, 1957), 266—index entry for "Nuestra Señora del Carmen."

15. Chávez, *But Time and Chance*, 15–16; and Margaret L. Buxton, comp., *The Family of Lucero de Godoi: Early Records* (Albuquerque: New Mexico Genealogical Society, 1981), 86.

16. Three of her siblings were baptized at Cochití: María Guadalupe (1766), Julian Hermenigildo (1768), and Juan Carlos (1771). Buxton, *The Family of Lucero de Godoi*, 86. The absence of an entry for the baptism of María del Carmel in the Cochití church records suggests, although does not prove, her birth elsewhere. Since the family later lived in Abiquiú, where baptismal records are spottier for the years before 1777, that seems like the likely place (see Chávez, *Archives of the Archdiocese*, 200). The census of circa 1790 puts her age at seventeen, suggesting that she was born about 1773. Her parents do not appear in that census. Olmsted, *Spanish and Mexican Censuses*, 117.

17. Ross Frank, "From Settler to Citizen: Economic Development and Cultural Change in Late Colonial New Mexico, 1750–1820" (Ph.D. diss., University of California, Berkeley, 1992), 40–57.

18. Ibid., 64–67.

19. Chávez, *But Time and Chance*, 15, who cites the marriage record in AASF, M–1, B–10, Abiquiú. For Severino's age, see above, n. 7; the age of María del Carmel can be extrapolated from the 1790 census, which lists her as seventeen.

20. Marc Simmons, *Coronado's Land: Essays on Daily Life in Colonial New Mexico* (Albuquerque: University of New Mexico Press, 1991), 13, 18.

21. Minge, "Last Will and Testament," 37.

22. Ibid.

23. Victor Westphall, *Mercedes Reales: Hispanic Land Grants of the Upper Río Grande Region* (Albuquerque: University of New Mexico Press, 1983), 199–200.

24. Olmsted, *Spanish and Mexican Censuses*, 114, 117. Chávez, *But Time and Chance*, 15, who cites AASF, M–1, B–10, Abiquiú. Swadesh, *Los Primeros Pobladores*, 44, identifies San Miguel as near present-day Cañones. Paul Kutsche and John R. Van Ness, *Cañones: Values, Crisis, and Survival in a Northern New Mexico Village* (Albuquerque: University of New Mexico Press, 1981), 15, located it at Barranca, west of Abiquiú, which historian John O. Baxter regards as an error since San José rather than San Miguel is the patron of that village. Baxter suggests that San Miguel might have been today's La Puente. Baxter to Weber, Santa Fe, August 29, 1994.

25. F. Stanley [Stanley F. Crocchiola], *The Abiquiu (New Mexico) Story* (n.p.: [1961?]), 1.

26. See Marc Simmons, *Witchcraft on the Río Grande: Spanish and Indian Supernaturalism in New Mexico* (Flagstaff: Northland Press, 1974). Swadesh, *Los Primeros Pobladores*, 44, associates witchcraft at Abiquiú with *genízaros*.

27. Kutsche and Van Ness, *Cañones*, 23.

28. "*de clase nobles.*" Antonio José Martínez, *Relación de Méritos del Presbítero Antonio José Martínez . . . cura engargado de Taos en el Departamento de Nuevo Mexico* (Taos: Impresa de su oficina á cargo de Jesus Maria Baca, 1838), 3. See, too, the stiff translation by Cecil V. Romero, ed. and trans., "Apologia of Presbyter Antonio J. Martínez . . . 1838," *NMHR* 3 (October 1928):336.

29. This figure, 15.6 percent, derives from a study of 424 men who enlisted for military duty between 1732 and 1820. The figure for Santa Fe was higher—36.4 percent. Bernardo P. Gallegos, *Literacy, Education, and Society in New Mexico, 1693–1821* (Albuquerque: University of New Mexico Press, 1992), 52. Gallegos defines a literate person as one who could sign his or her name because reading was taught before writing in New Mexico (pp. 34–47). We know that Severino Martínez could sign his name.

30. Petition to Gov. Fernando de Chacón (circa 1797).

31. Severino Martín representing Rosa Martín, María Manuela Martín, José Manuel Martín, María Manuela Martín, Trinidad Martín, and Guadalupe Martín, heirs of Juan Martín and the widow Juana Trujillo [Abiquiú?], May 19, 1804. Gonzales Papers, Ayer Collection, no. 1097A, Newberry Library, Chicago, Illinois.

32. [Martínez], *Historia cons[c]isa.*

33. Gallegos, *Literacy, Education, and Society in New Mexico,* 21–39.

34. Tey Diana Rebolledo, "'Y Dónde Estaban las Mujeres?': In Pursuit of an *Hispana* Literary and Historical Heritage in Colonial New Mexico, 1580–1840," in María Herrera-Sobek, ed., *Reconstructing a Chicano/A Literary Heritage: Hispanic Colonial Literature of the Southwest* (Tucson: University of Arizona Press, 1993), 140–57.

35. Salazar, "Santa Rosa de Lima de Abiquiu," 18; and Adams and Chávez, *Missions of New Mexico, 1776,* 252–53.

36. For the restrictions, see Simmons, *Spanish Government,* 185.

37. Swadesh, *Los Primeros Pobladores,* 159–70.

38. Ibid., 43–48. For an unromantic view of the role of *genízaros,* see Ramón A. Gutiérrez, *When Jesus Came, the Corn Mothers Went Away: Marriage, Sexuality, and Power in New Mexico, 1500–1846* (Stanford: Stanford University Press, 1991), 171–90. In an otherwise fine discussion, Gutiérrez consistently equates *genízaros* with slaves—a condition that suggests an inherited quality of servitude, which was not the case for *genízaros.*

39. For a summary and guidance to sources, see David J. Weber, *The Spanish Frontier in North America* (New Haven: Yale University Press, 1992), 307–8, 466, n. 24.

40. John L. Kessell, "Sources for the History of a New Mexico Community: Abiquiú," *NMHR* 54 (October 1979):263.

41. The circa 1790 census distinguished clearly between the "pueblo" of Santo Tomás of Abiquiú and the surrounding "plazas," and the priest's entries in the baptismal book for the area in the 1790s distinguished between those infants born in the "pueblo" and those children of Hispanics whom he designated as *vecinos.*

42. Chávez, *But Time and Chance,* 16, reports that on October 23, 1779, Severino's mother, Micaela, is recorded in the baptismal register as godmother and owner of an eight-year-old Comanche girl.

43. Chávez, *But Time and Chance,* 16; and Minge, "Last Will and Testament," 36.

44. Ross Frank, "The Creation of a *Vecino* Culture in Late Colonial New Mexico, 1780-1820," in Virginia Guedea and Jaime E. Rodríguez O., eds., *Five Centuries of Mexican History,* 2 vols. (Mexico: Instituto Mora, 1992), 2:261, and his figure 3. Drawn from his Ph.D. dissertation, "From Settler to Citizen," Frank's article reinterprets the late eighteenth century as a time of dynamic growth for New Mexico.

45. Frank, "From Settler to Citizen," 197.

46. Weber, *Spanish Frontier,* 230–34.

47. Frank, "Creation of a *Vecino* Culture," 256; and Frank, "From Settler to Citizen," 146–52.

48. Marc Simmons, ed. and trans., "The Chacón Economic Report of 1803," *NMHR* 60 (January 1985):88.

49. Frank, "Creation of a *Vecino* Culture," 254–61.

50. Weber, *Spanish Frontier,* 235.

51. Frank, "Creation of a *Vecino* Culture," 261.

52. Adams and Chávez, eds. and trans., *Missions of*

New Mexico, 1776, 126. At this time, Santa Rosa de Lima and Santa Rosa Capilla—distinct places in the 1790 census—may have been a single community.

53. Olmsted, *Spanish and Mexican Censuses*, 111–121; Swadesh, *Los Primeros Pobladores*, 46.

54. Salazar, "Santa Rosa de Lima de Abiquiu," 18, suggests that a growing population in the region apparently strained the limits of arable land around Santa Rosa, leading some residents to move away.

55. Most notably Sebastián Martín of Santa Cruz de la Cañada, but relationships remain hypothetical. Genealogies need to be further developed.

56. Minge, "Last Will and Testament," 37.

57. Howard Roberts Lamar, *The Far Southwest, 1846–1912: A Territorial History* (New Haven: Yale University Press, 1966), 39. The relationships that Lamar asserted now need to be demonstrated and clarified. For example, the family of Severino Martínez and José Manuel Martínez do not seem to be related, as Lamar supposed (p. 38). Nonetheless, the "web of consanguinity" woven by don Severino's relatives does seem to have stretched over a large territory.

CHAPTER
❖ TWO

A Landed Estate in Taos

THE TAOS VALLEY runs north and south, flanked by the deep gorge of the Río Grande to the west and mountains to the south, east, and north. Visitors found it enchanting. Antonio Barreiro, a Mexican lawyer who came to New Mexico in 1831, wrote of it: "This valley is doubtless one of the most beautiful and fertile sections of the territory."[1] Josiah Gregg, an American merchant who traded extensively in New Mexico in the 1830s, was more emphatic: "No part of New Mexico equals this valley in amenity of soil, richness of produce and beauty of appearance. Whatever is thrown into its prolific bosom . . . grows to a wonderful degree of perfection."[2] Severino Martínez had brought his family to a place whose climate and soil allowed them to prosper. "In years of drought or of crop failures," Barreiro wrote, "the valley of Taos furnishes supplies to all of New Mexico, and the settlers always have enough left for their maintenance."[3]

Taos

Hispanic settlers in the Taos Valley lived at the farthest edge of the *camino real*—the king's highway—that ran north from Mexico City.[4] Taos was some seventy miles north of Santa Fe over the most direct road, one that followed the Río

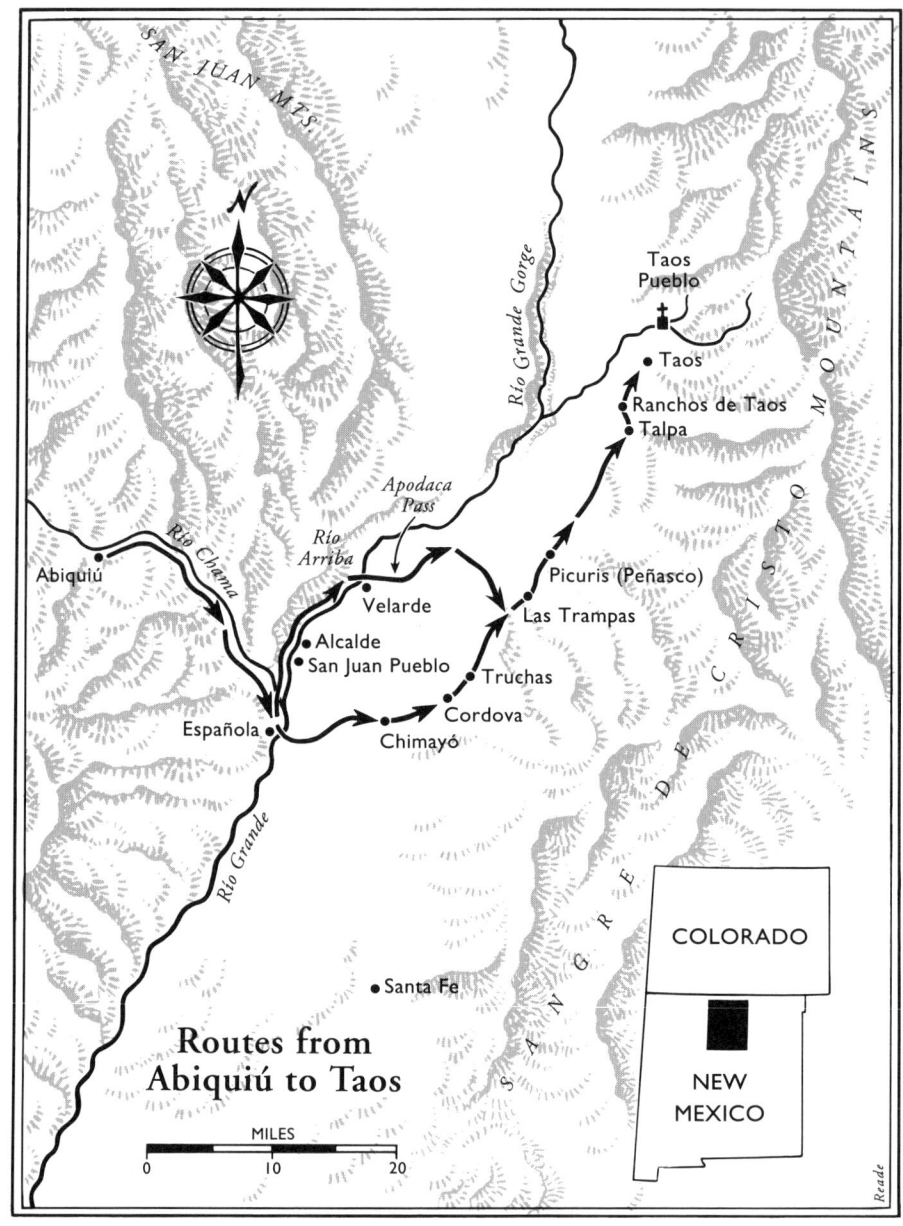

Grande. A canyon north of present Velarde, however, was "barely wide enough for horses to pass"[5] and made the direct route impractical for those driving ox carts or herds. Drovers skirted the narrow canyon by following the more roundabout Apodaca Pass route or by taking the still lengthier summer road (today's "high road") that took one from Taos through Talpa, Peñasco, Trampas, Truchas, and Chimayó before returning to the Río Grande and descending to Santa Fe.[6]

When the Martínez family moved to Taos in 1804, the valley would have seemed as remote and raw a frontier as their old village on the Chama, but, in fact, Taos had been home to apartment-dwelling farmers for at least a half millennium. In the fifteenth century Tiwa-speaking Indians had begun to build the magnificent multistoried pueblo of Taos at the north end of the Taos Valley at the site it still occupies today. Spaniards first saw this northernmost pueblo when one of Francisco Vázquez de Coronado's lieutenants visited it in 1540.[7] Not until the mid-1600s, though, did Spanish colonists settle that far north beyond their capital at Santa Fe. Then, they came in small numbers. By 1680 only seventy of New Mexico's twenty-eight hundred *vecinos*, or Hispanic residents, lived in the valley.[8]

That year Hispanic New Mexico collapsed. *Vecinos* had built new lives in New Mexico at the expense of the Pueblos, exploiting their land and labor; Spanish Franciscans had tried to suppress expressions of native religious faith. In the explosion remembered as the Pueblo Revolt of 1680, Pueblos drove Hispanics out of all of New Mexico, sending a stream of homeless refugees southward toward El Paso.[9]

Led by don Diego de Vargas, Hispanic colonists began to reconquer New Mexico in 1692, but not until 1715 did they reestablish civil government in the Taos Valley or begin to resettle there.[10] At first, they started farms instead of towns, preferring life on scattered homesteads, or *ranchos*, where they could watch over their fields and stock. Dismayed government officials argued the wisdom of living in communities for mutual protection, and their concerns often proved well warranted, as *vecinos* in the Taos Valley discovered.[11] When raids by Comanches intensified in the 1750s, defenseless Hispanics had to abandon their *ranchos* and move into the well-fortified Taos Pueblo, alongside the Indians. Bishop Pedro Tamarón of Durango, who inspected the "spacious and beautiful" Taos Valley in 1760, found that thirty-six Hispanic families, numbering 160 people, had moved into the Indian pueblo, living alongside 159 Indian families—a total of some 505 people. Much of the *vecino* population of the Taos Valley continued to live in the pueblo into the 1780s.[12]

In the mid-1770s a new Hispanic community began to take shape toward the south end of the valley at today's Ranchos de Taos, but not until the mid-1780s, when threats from Comanches and Navajos had diminished, did *vecinos* settle at the site of present-day Taos. Three miles south of the Taos Pueblo, on Indian land, squatters settled on the Río Fernando de Taos, named after a seventeenth-century settler, don Fernando de Chávez. Over time, the village took the name of the river, along with various other names—Don Fernando, Don Fernández, San Fernando, and San Fernández de Taos.[13]

The plaza of Don Fernando de Taos, which became the center of the valley's Hispanic life, came into being officially in 1796. That year Gov. Fernando de Chacón authorized the *alcalde* of the pueblo of Taos, Antonio José Ortiz, to put sixty-three families in possession of a grant of communal land—the Don Fernando de Taos grant. Ortiz followed the traditional procedure:

❖

I took them by the hand and proclaimed in clear and intelligible words, that in the name of His Majesty—God preserve Him—and without prejudice to his royal interest or that of any third party, I led them over Said tract and they plucked up grass, cast stone, taking possession of said lands quietly and peaceably . . . and shouted aloud, long live the King.[14]

Danger from Indians may have diminished but had not disappeared. As a condition for receiving the land, each settler had to possess arms—bows and arrows or firearms; within two years, everyone had to own a firearm or "be ejected" from the settlement.

Even before the official granting of land at Don Fernando de Taos in 1796, the community had a population of 195 persons. By then, a few families of *vecinos* had also settled nearby in five other small plazas. To the southwest of Don Fernando, along the Río del Pueblo, sixty-one persons lived at the Plaza de la Purísma (known today as Upper Ranchitos), and another sixty-three people lived at the Plaza de San Francisco de Paula (Lower Ranchitos), where Severino Martínez would relocate his family. Eighty-six people lived to the southeast of Don Fernando at the Plaza de Nuestra Señora de los Dolores (today's Cañón). Due south of Don Fernando, Ranchos de Taos (then the Plaza de San Francisco) rivaled it in population, with 191 *vecinos*—as did the neighborhood of La Loma (then the Plaza de Santa Gertrudis), with 183.[15]

These six plazas apparently came into being as a small stream of *vecinos* moved into the Taos Valley following the mid-1780s thaw in Spanish-Comanche

San Francisco de Paula.
Collection of Larry Frank, Taos.

relations. From a population recorded at 308 in 1789, the number of Hispanics in the Taos Valley had risen to 783 by 1800.[16] Nonetheless, the six plazas in the valley lacked the basic amenities of a town, including a resident priest.

As in many small New Mexican villages, residents of Don Fernando had not been able to receive the sacraments of their faith unless a priest traveled to them or they traveled some distance to the priest. Three miles separated Don Fernando from the mission church of San Gerónimo, where the same resident Franciscan who served the Indian pueblo of Taos also ministered to the Hispanic residents of the valley.

Although Don Fernando de Taos lacked a resident priest in 1804, it may have had a little church, or *capilla*. On September 18, 1801, in response to a request from residents of Don Fernando, the bishop of Durango had authorized construction of a chapel to be dedicated to Nuestra Señora de Guadalupe. When that chapel was completed or consecrated is not clear, but by 1815 the

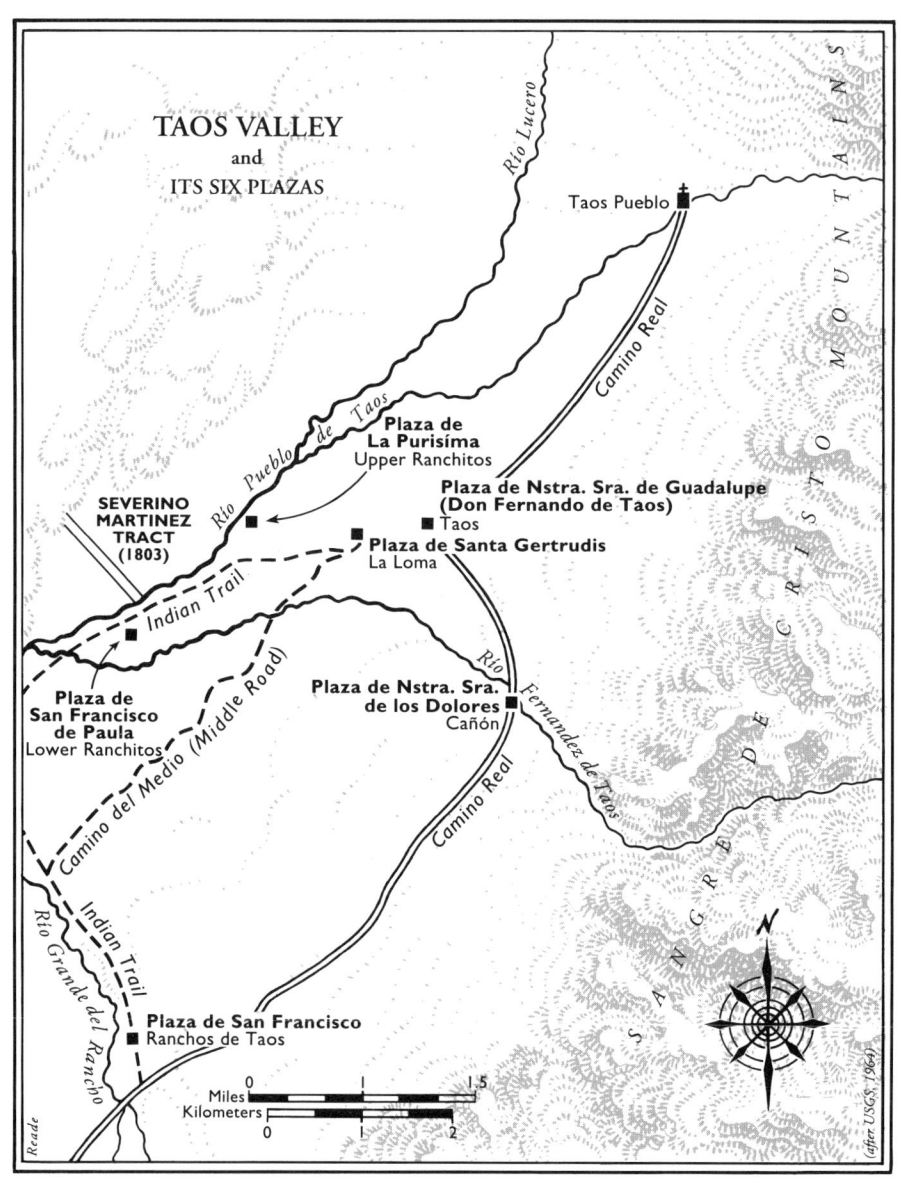

chapel of Nuestra Señora de Guadalupe at Don Fernando had become an "*ayuda de parroquia*," an auxiliary chapel to the church of San Gerónimo. Comanche attacks, it was said, had made the road between Don Fernando and the Indian pueblo dangerous, and so the Franciscan priest at Taos Pueblo would travel regularly (but not necessarily weekly) to say Mass in the village rather than have the villagers come to him.[17]

For the remainder of don Severino's life, the same priest who ministered to the Taos Indian Pueblo also served the village of Don Fernando de Taos. Pueblo Indians and *vecinos* alike belonged to the parish of San Gerónimo, with the Indian church of San Gerónimo de Taos functioning as the parish headquarters until 1826. Following the completion of the chapel of Guadalupe, though, Pueblos and Hispanos worshiped apart in the Taos Valley, just as they lived apart.[18]

To this place so old and yet so new, so rough-edged and yet so promising, Severino and María Martínez brought their family of three children from Abiquiú: the eldest a son, Antonio José (born on January 17, 1793),[19] and two daughters, María Estefana (born January 1, 1797) and Juana María (born July 26, 1799).[20] During their early years in Taos, Severino and María would have three more children, all boys: José María de Jesús, José Santiago, and Juan Pascual Bailon.

These six children lived into adulthood, giving Severino and María a family twice as large as the norm for their parents' generation.[21] The survival of so many of their children into adulthood may have reflected the growing affluence of their family, as well as an improved diet. Then, too, smallpox had begun to be eradicated. Six years after its discovery in 1799 by Edward Jenner and a year after the Martínez family had settled in Taos, the smallpox vaccine had reached New Mexico. Transported as cowpox in the bodies of children, the vaccine was widely administered.[22]

Since Taos lacked a school as well as a church in its early years, the Martínez children apparently studied on their own. Antonio José, who had learned to read and write at school in Abiquiú at age five, remembered that he read, wrote, and learned mathematics on his own at Taos.[23] Don Severino apparently encouraged his sons, if not his daughters, to learn to read and write; Juan Pascual, the youngest, attained sufficient education to become a judge.[24]

Land and labor

Whatever brought him to Taos, Severino took advantage of his new circumstances to become one of the valley's wealthiest citizens and most prominent public officials. We know little of his first years in the valley, but it is clear that Severino "Martín," as he then called himself, bought a tract of land there from Antonio Archuleta on October 2, 1803, and that he and his family moved to the Taos Valley in March 1804.[25]

The land that don Severino selected lay two miles southwest of Don Fernando at the smaller plaza of San Francisco de Paula del Ranchito—known simply as San Francisco del Ranchito or more simply as Ranchitos.[26] His original property measured sixty varas along the Río del Pueblo, which bounded it on the southeast as it flowed southwesterly toward the Río Grande from its source in the Sangre de Cristo Mountains near Taos Pueblo. Suitable for growing wheat ("*tierra de pan llevar*"), this land extended to the ridge ("*la ceja*") that can be seen today on the western horizon from the Martínez house. To the southwest it abutted the land of Joaquín Martín and to the northeast the lands of the seller, Antonio Archuleta. According to family tradition, a four-room house stood on the property, which Severino and María Martínez would add to over the years.[27]

The availability of water may have influenced don Severino's decision to locate at Ranchitos rather than at Don Fernando. Several years before the Martínez family moved to the Taos Valley, water from the Río Fernando de Taos that flows through Don Fernando had already proved inadequate for local Hispanic settlers.[28] Small farmers, however, had also settled along the Río del Pueblo, on the old Gijosa land grant, south of the Don Fernando grant, and had begun to irrigate. Sometime between 1745 and 1800, *vecinos* had constructed two substantial irrigation ditches, the Pacheco and the San Francisco de Paula.[29] Don Severino would have found the Río del Pueblo and the nearby ditches, or *acequias*, a great attraction, as was the Río Fernando de Taos, to which some of his land soon extended.

If the Martínez family had left Santa Rosa de Lima de Abiquiú in search of more land for fields and flocks, they found it in Taos and environs. In subsequent years, don Severino augmented his holdings by purchasing additional parcels from his neighbors, as in 1811 when he bought 143 varas of land for growing wheat from José Antonio Lobato. That parcel, too, ran along the Río del Pueblo, which was its southern boundary, and extended northerly to the Río Grande; on the "west," the parcel adjoined Severino's own property, and on the "east," it bordered on land belonging to Juana Trujillo.[30]

By the time of his death in 1827, don Severino owned five large tracts along the Río del Pueblo. Two of those tracts extended eastward over a low-lying, well-watered area to what is still today called the Camino del Medio, the middle road. A fifth tract ran 409 varas (nearly the length of four football fields) along the Río del Pueblo up to the Río Lucero and stretched westward from the Río del Pueblo toward the Río Grande, "as far as the right may be."[31]

As their property grew, Severino and María Martínez might have come to think of their contiguous landholdings as an "hacienda"—the term a later generation applied to his house rather than to his properties. In modern parlance in the Southwest we commonly imagine a certain type of house to be an "hacienda,"[32] but the word "hacienda" in its classical sense in Mexico referred to an entire estate with its extensive lands and its buildings, or *casco*, including barns, stables, corrals, chapel, dwellings for workers and managers (sometimes entire villages), and the great manor house itself. In their classic form, haciendas reflected heavy investment in capital improvements, employed large numbers of laborers, and oriented production toward large markets. Contrary to an older conventional wisdom, haciendas were not, nor were they intended to be, self-sufficient. Their proprietors depended on markets and often on outside income.

Since New Mexico's modest export economy could not support the large estates of central Mexico, some specialists have doubted that haciendas existed in Spanish Colonial New Mexico.[33] Size and diversity of operations usually distinguished haciendas from *estancias* or *ranchos*, but the difference between an hacienda, an estancia, and a rancho was never firmly drawn. Size and the complexity of operations were relative to the local economy,[34] and in relation to other landholdings in New Mexico, the Martínez estate was sizable enough that contemporaries might well have known it as an hacienda.

Whatever they called it, the Martínez clan operated a family ranching and farming operation that was quite large by the standards of Río Arriba (Hispanic New Mexico north of Santa Fe). New Mexico's large estates tended to cluster in the Río Abajo, the area below Santa Fe, where the floodplain of the Río Grande widened. To the north, in the view of the *abajeños*, lived poor cousins.

Beyond his contiguous lands along the Río del Pueblo, Severino Martínez also acquired interests in property beyond Don Fernando de Taos, as Hispanic pioneers pushed northward beyond the Taos Valley. In the spring of 1815 he was one of a group of more than forty settlers scheduled to receive an interest in a new community land grant at Arroyo Hondo (a José and a Juana Martín, who may have been his son and daughter, were also among them). As was customary with community grants, each grantee received a standard-size lot for a house and a piece of farmland; the entire community held the remaining grazing and woodlands in common. At the cutting edge of Hispanic settlement, twelve miles to the northwest of Taos, Arroyo Hondo was a dangerous place in 1815. Settlers who did not come equipped with a gun would not qualify for land. Some of the grantees began to plant, fence, and build a small plaza that spring, but there is no evidence that Severino joined them. As a landowner, Severino had no right to own part of a community grant, which the law reserved for landless settlers. Still, that alone does not explain Martínez's absence, for local officials often overlooked the law in order to look after friends and family.35

Severino Martínez apparently maintained his interest in Arroyo Hondo for the remainder of his life. In 1825, when he served as alcalde of Taos, eight petitioners asked him to grant them vacant land on the Arroyo Hondo. Martínez honored their request, giving each 128 varas of land and rewarding himself with fifty varas for his trouble.36 When he drew up his will in 1827, he noted that he owned land at Arroyo Hondo, one hundred varas "in width and in length from the river to the ridge." Since he also owned a "middle-sized room in the house of my niece Trinidad Salazar" at the plaza of Arroyo Hondo, as he noted in his will, it seems likely that he visited there to oversee work on his property or at another piece of real estate that he held nearby.37

In 1815, the same year the original Arroyo Hondo grant was made, Gov. Alberto Máynez also ordered the alcalde of Taos, Pablo Lucero, to grant don Severino farming land on San Cristóbal Creek—some two miles north of Arroyo Hondo. After ascertaining that such a grant would not prejudice the rights of any third party, Alcalde Lucero, his witnesses, and Severino Martínez traveled to the site on October 8, 1815. There, Lucero performed the legal rituals that put don Severino in possession of the land. Although his employees may have farmed the land or grazed herds at San Cristóbal, don Severino did not maintain a house there. Spanish law required a grantee to live for four years on a grant in order to perfect title. Perhaps for that reason, as well as the impropriety of claiming interest in two land grants, Martínez did not list the property in his will. Whatever the case, when his heirs divided up the estate, his wife received the tract of land at San Cristóbal.38 After the United States occupied New Mexico, the Martínez heirs claimed an interest in the San Cristóbal grant, dropping their claim only after the U.S. Surveyor General denied its validity in 1878.39

Don Severino's motives for acquiring more land seem clear. He sought to expand his farming operations in the river bottoms and increase the size of his herds and flocks that grazed on the dry mesas. Like others in the Taos Valley, a valley of farmers and ranchers, don Severino grew wheat, corn, and perhaps a variety of other crops, such as peas, beans, and pumpkins;40 in addition, he raised livestock, especially sheep.

The number of sheep in the province had risen dramatically over the course of don Severino's lifetime. In 1757, four years before he was born, New Mexico had an estimated fifty thousand sheep; when Severino Martínez died in 1827, the number had risen to nearly 240,000.⁴¹ Sheep were the mainstay of the New Mexico ranching economy, especially in the Río Abajo. New Mexicans apparently preferred sheep, a tough little breed called a *churro*, over cattle and horses in part because they were more likely to survive drought and because their slowness and resistance to stampeding made them less attractive to Indian raiders.⁴² Martínez's choice of stock reflected the larger pattern of ownership in New Mexico. At the time of his death, he owned 1,152 sheep, 60 goats, 62 horses (36 of them still unbroken), 60 head of cattle, 28 mules, 9 burros, 41 oxen, and 6 pigs.⁴³ Throughout New Mexico in 1827, *vecinos* and Pueblo Indians owned livestock in similar proportions: 240,000 sheep and goats compared to only 5,000 cattle, 2,150 mules, and 850 horses.⁴⁴

As Martínez's lands, herds, and flocks grew, so did his need for labor. Judging from his prosperity, don Severino met that need. Like many New Mexicans who raised sheep, he may have employed herders through a system that resembled a bank loan, with livestock substituting for money. Under that system herders agreed to guard and breed a flock of borrowed sheep for a specified period of time, then return the borrowed animals in the same condition they had received them, together with interest payments of ewes and lambs. With luck, the herders, or *partidarios*, received a share, or *partido*, of the newborn animals and eventually built up their own flocks and prospered. Unfortunately, in bad times, herders might be unable to repay the loan, much less the interest. Some would fall into permanent debt to *patrones*, such as don Severino, and become tied to their estates.⁴⁵

Like his father before him, Severino Martínez probably employed *genízaro* servants. On April 8, 1810, there is record of the baptism of María, an eight-year-old Ute girl, "ransomed by Severino Martín."⁴⁶ It also appears that the part-Indian woman, María Gertrudis, who might have been Severino's half sister, joined the family at Taos. In his will in 1827, Severino characterized a María Gertrudis as a former housekeeper (*fámula*) now married; he left her a large tract of land, as he did another former housekeeper, one María Dolores, who might have been the eight-year-old Ute girl, now grown and married.⁴⁷ Other *genízaros* could have worked for the family without leaving a trace in the meager documentary records. We know, for example, that don Severino tried with or without success to acquire a ransomed Indian girl in a deal in 1816.⁴⁸

Just as relations between white masters and black slaves in the American South varied with the individuals, so too did Hispano-*genízaro* relationships in New Mexico. Whatever the ambience in which they worked, be it one of beatings and humiliation or of respect as a family member, *genízaros* generally did the most menial household chores. Historian Ramón A. Gutiérrez vividly describes the tasks of women household servants, or *genízaras:*

> *Corn had to be shucked and wheat threshed, ground into flour, and baked into bread. Chili peppers had to be tied into riestras [ristras] and hung out to dry. Any meat that was not immediately consumed after a slaughter had to be salted and dried into jerky. There were buildings to construct and to plaster—all women's work. When not otherwise caring for household needs female slaves [genízaras] undertook production for the market. Animal pelts had to be tanned and sewn into shoes and saddles. Cotton and wool were spun and knit into socks, gloves, and caps, or woven into blankets and rugs, all of which would be sold in Chihuahua for manufactured goods and luxury items.*[49]

In frontier Taos, family members must have also pitched in to share the daily chores. It seems unlikely that even the *ricos* in the Taos Valley "lived pleasant lazy lives" with peones doing all of their work, as one popular writer imagined, or that this was a "halcyon period . . . the Days of the Dons."[50] Antonio José Martínez, age eleven when his family moved to Taos, later recalled the work of his youth on his family's properties. He remembered gathering firewood in the hills and watching cattle in the summers. After he turned fourteen, he helped with the heavier farm work, hauled goods as a muleteer, or *arriero*, and occasionally took charge of the family's distant rural holdings.[51]

Like other women of her station, doña María del Carmel must have assumed responsibility for running the domestic side of the hacienda: for planting the household garden, for harvesting and preserving food for winter, for making candles and soap, for weaving fabrics for clothing, bedding, and carpets, for the daily menu, and for care and training of the children in sickness and in health. As one writer has noted:

> *Planning for the replacement of furnishings, directing the plastering done in the spring and fall, all of the management of the houses*

that assumed the proportions of modern institutions, such as hotels and hospitals, fell to the lot of the doñas. . . . The challenges of daily life were enormous, and added to these were the bearing of children, and the social duties that befitted women of their station in life.[52]

However hard members of the Martínez family worked in their new surroundings, though, life beyond the subsistence level depended on commerce and the availability of markets.

Notes

1. Antonio Barreiro, *Ojeada sobre Nuevo-Mejico* (1832), in H. Bailey Carroll and J. Villasana Haggard, eds. and trans., *Three New Mexico Chronicles* . . . (Albuquerque: The Quivira Society, 1942), 86–87. For earlier comments, see John O. Baxter, *Spanish Irrigation in Taos Valley* (Santa Fe: New Mexico State Engineer Office, 1990), 10–15.

2. Josiah Gregg, *Commerce of the Prairies*, Max L. Moorhead, ed. (1st ed., 1844; Norman: University of Oklahoma Press, 1954), 104.

3. Barreiro, *Ojeada*, 87.

4. Marc Simmons, *Spanish Government in New Mexico* (Albuquerque: University of New Mexico Press, 1968), 73.

5. Barreiro, *Ojeada*, 31.

6. Helen G. Blumenschein, "Historic Roads & Trails to Taos," *El Palacio* 75 (Spring 1968):9–19.

7. John J. Bodine, "Taos Pueblo," in Alfonso Ortiz, ed., *Southwest*, vol. 9, *Handbook of North American Indians*, William C. Sturtevant, ed. (Washington, D.C.: Smithsonian Institution, 1979), 255–67. Taoseños had begun to build *near* the site in 1350.

8. Charles Wilson Hackett, ed., *Revolt of the Pueblo Indians and Otermín's Attempted Reconquest, 1680–1682*, Charmion Clair Shelby, trans., 2 vols. (Albuquerque: University of New Mexico Press, 1941), 1:xx, xxx.

9. For a brief introduction to these events, see David J. Weber, *The Spanish Frontier in North America* (New Haven: Yale University Press, 1992), chapters 4 and 5.

10. Baxter, *Spanish Irrigation in Taos Valley*, 5. Much of this discussion is drawn from Baxter, the best account of early Taos, and Myra Ellen Jenkins, "Taos Pueblo and Its Neighbors, 1540–1847," *NMHR* 41 (April 1966):85–114.

11. Marc Simmons, "Settlement Patterns and Village Plans in New Mexico," in David J. Weber, ed., *New Spain's Far Northern Frontier: Essays on Spain in the American West* (Albuquerque: University of New Mexico Press, 1979), 97–115.

12. Eleanor B. Adams, ed. and trans., *Bishop Tamarón's Visitation of New Mexico, 1760* (Albuquerque: Historical Society of New Mexico, 1954), 56–57.

13. T. M. Pierce, ed., assisted by Ina Sizer Cassidy and Helen S. Pearce, *New Mexico Place Names: A Geographical Dictionary* (Albuquerque: University of New Mexico Press, 1965), 162. Josiah Gregg noted in 1844 that there was no town called "Taos" but only the Valley of Taos, which contained several villages, including "Fernandez and Los Ranchos." *Commerce of the Prairies*, 104.

14. Rowena Martínez, ed., *Land Grants in Taos Valley: Quotations From Original Source Material* (Taos: Taos County Historical Society, 1968), 11.

15. Baxter, *Spanish Irrigation in Taos Valley*, 17–18; Baxter has since identified Santa Gertrudis (letter to Weber, August 29, 1994).

16. Ross Frank, "From Settler to Citizen: Economic Development and Cultural Change in Late Colonial New Mexico, 1750–1820" (Ph.D. diss., University of California, Berkeley, 1992), 199–200, 417–18. Of the 1,314 residents of the valley in 1800, 531 were Pueblo Indians. The remaining 783 appear in the census under Don Fernando but presumably include nearby plazas that fell within the same jurisdiction.

17. Angélico Chávez, *Archives of the Archdiocese of Santa Fe, 1678–1900* (Washington, D.C.: Academy of Franciscan History, 1957), 156, describing the contents of Book XV, Box 6, Taos. Santiago Valdez, "Biography of Padre Antonio José Martínez, cura-pastor of Parish of Taos, N.Mex., A.D. 1877, by Santiago Valdez," Rev. Juan Romero, trans. (unpublished manuscript, 1993), 102–3, reproduces the bishop's authorization of 1801, which refers to the petition to build the chapel. Angélico Chávez, *But Time and Chance: The Story of Padre Martínez of Taos, 1793–1867* (Santa Fe: Sunstone Press, 1981), 28, supposes that work began on the chapel in the spring of 1802.

18. In his will, don Severino identified himself as a resident of the "plaza de San Fernando de San Geronimo de Taos." Ward Alan Minge, ed. and trans., "The Last Will and Testament of Don Severino Martínez," *New Mexico Quarterly* 33 (Spring 1963):40, 41. See, too, the burial records of Severino Martínez and María del Carmel Martínez, cited later in chapter 7. New Mexicans used the term "parish" to describe Taos even before it was officially secularized. See Pedro Bautista Pino's *Exposición* (1812) in Carroll and Haggard, *Three New Mexico Chronicles* . . . , 50, 236.

19. Chávez, *But Time and Chance*, 13, reports on the baptismal record and explains that the "birth certificate" described by the biographer of Antonio José, Santiago Valdez, is a fake. The fake is reproduced in the addendum to Fred G. Martínez, *The Story of Antonio Severino Martínez y Lucero de Godoy and María del Carmel Santistevan* (Taos: Kit Carson Memorial Foundation Publications in History, no. 6, 1977).

20. The transcriptions of all three children's baptisms (with birth dates) are most readily accessible in "Abiquiu Baptisms, 1754–1866," a database prepared by Thomas D. Martínez and various members of the Genealogical Society of New Mexico. This may be consulted at the New Mexico State Records Center and Archives. I am grateful to archivist Sandra Jaramillo, who sent me a copy of the relevant pages, as well as photocopies of the original baptismal entries.

21. Alicia V. Tjarks, "Demographic, Ethnic, and Occupational Structure of New Mexico, 1790," *The Americas* 35 (July 1978):71–72; and David J. Weber, *The Mexican Frontier, 1821–1846: The American Southwest under Mexico* (Albuquerque: University of New Mexico Press, 1982), 218.

22. Lansing Bartlett Bloom, *Early Vaccination in New Mexico* (Santa Fe: Historical Society of New Mexico, [1925], publication no. 27).

23. [Antonio José Martínez], *Historia cons[c]isa del cura de Taos Antonio José Martínez* (Taos: Vicente F. Romero, 1861), 1; and Chávez, *But Time and Chance*, 17, 27. Chávez dates the first school at 1819.

24. Judge of the Second District of Arroyo Hondo in 1835. J. J. Bowden, "Private Land Claims in the Southwest," 6 vols. (LL.M. [master of laws] thesis, Southern Methodist University, 1969) 4:932.

25. The deed of sale, cited below in n. 27. Sources for Martínez moving to the Taos Valley from Abiquiú in 1804 are: his own statement in his will, and [Martínez], *Historia cons[c]isa del cura de Taos*, 1, which gives the month as well as the year. Bainbridge Bunting, *Taos Adobes: Spanish Colonial and Territorial Architecture of the Taos Valley* (Santa Fe: Fort Burgwin Research Center and Museum of New Mexico Press, 1964), 23, and Bainbridge Bunting, *Early Architecture in New Mexico* (Albuquerque: University of New Mexico Press, 1976), 63, assert that Martínez acquired the property in 1824—an error that other writers apparently have taken from Bunting and repeated. Antonio Archuleta has not been identified, but an Antonio Archuleta was among the recipients of the Arroyo Hondo grant, along with Severino Martínez. See, below, n. 35.

26. The copy of the bill of sale of 1803, cited below, refers to it as "San Francisco de Padua in Ranchito"—perhaps a transcriber's misreading of "Paula." In his will, Martínez refers to his neighborhood as "San Francisco del Ranchito."

27. The deed of sale from Antonio Archuleta to Severino Martín mentions only land, *not* structures—see below, chapter 8, for identification of these rooms. Deed Records of Taos County, New

Mexico, vol. A–20, p. 546, filed in 1911. Translation in Northern New Mexico Abstract and Title Company, Taos, New Mexico, Abstract of Title, no. A–597. Xerox copies of both Spanish transcription and English translation in KCHM. Juan Manuel Martínez, a great-grandson of Severino (and son of Agapito Martínez), told Guadalupe Baca Vaughn that Severino's family lived on the east side of the Río del Pueblo, in the Plaza of San Francisco de Paula, when they first moved to Taos, and he showed Mrs. Vaughn the house. Telephone interview with Mrs. Vaughn, July 14, 1994.

28. Baxter, *Spanish Irrigation in Taos Valley*, 17, 70, finds the shortage as early as 1797.

29. Ibid., 80–81.

30. Deed Records of Taos County, New Mexico, vol. A–20, p. 548, a document dated July 9, 1811, representing the sale to Severino Martín of agricultural lands owned by José Antonio Lobato, bounded on the "south" by the "Río del Pueblo," which Lobato sold to Severino Martín for $210 (the English translation is very poor; I have consulted the Spanish-language transcription in the deed book).

31. Minge, "Last Will and Testament," 38, 47, 51. This latter piece, Martínez said, was "contained in four deeds." For "camino del medio," see the original Spanish-language version of the will. Reconstructing the precise boundaries of don Severino's tracts may be impossible since the Río del Pueblo no longer runs in the same channel that it did in the early nineteenth century.

32. The convention of using *casa grande* and hacienda as synonyms is well established in New Mexico. See, for example, E. Boyd, *Popular Arts of Spanish New Mexico* (Santa Fe: Museum of New Mexico Press, 1974), 5, who speaks of building "large, rambling haciendas," and Bunting, *Early Architecture*, 60, who equates an "hacienda" with a large house "built around two courtyards." The word may be misapplied, but its use is so well established in English that it seems likely to endure. See, too, Simmons, "Settlement Patterns," 107, and Fran Levine, "Hispanic Household Structure in Colonial New Mexico," in Bradley J. Vierra and Clara Gualtieri, eds., *Current Research on the Late Prehistory and Early History of New Mexico* (Albuquerque: New Mexico Archaeological Council Special Publication 1, July 1992), 197.

33. Philip Riley Bartholomew, "The Hacienda: Its Evolvement and Architecture in Colonial New Mexico, 1598–1821" (Ph.D. diss., University of Missouri, Columbia, 1983). Bartholomew takes a rigid view and concludes that "classic" haciendas did not exist in New Mexico; Jeff Girard wonders if they existed in the Taos Valley: "Historic Cultural Diversity and the Archaeology of the Taos Area," in Vierra and Gualtieri, *Current Research*, 335. David H. Snow, "A Review of Spanish Colonial Archaeology in Northern New Mexico: 'Where We're At, As They Say,'" in Vierra and Gualtieri, *Current Research*, 185–94, sees them as an eighteenth-century phenomenon.

34. Eric Van Young, *Hacienda and Market in Eighteenth-Century Mexico: The Rural Economy of the Guadalajara Region, 1675–1820* (Berkeley: University of California Press, 1981), 110–13; D. A. Brading, *Haciendas and Ranchos in the Mexican Bajío: León, 1700–1860* (New York: Cambridge University Press, 1978), 21. Leslie Offutt makes the point in her soon-to-be-published study of colonial Saltillo that the line between ranchos and haciendas confused even contemporaries. For the relative nature of definitions see *Noticias varias de Nueva Galicia, Intendencia de Guadalajara* (Guadalajara, 1878), 195, 198; this reference is courtesy of my colleague William Taylor.

35. Severino's name appears on the first of two lists of acts of possession, one dated April 6. In the four days separating those lists he may have withdrawn from the project. His daughter's name appears on both lists. Malcolm Ebright, "History of the Arroyo Hondo Grant," entered as testimony in *Montoya* v. *Anderson*, Taos County civil case no. 79–106, pp. 2–4. I am grateful to counselor Ebright for providing me with this piece and for guidance to other sources regarding Martínez's holdings. See, too, Ralph L. Hayes, comp., *Taos County, New Mexico: Materials Published in the New Mexico Genealogist, 1962–1988* (Albuquerque: New Mexico Genealogical Society, 1989), 115, 120. The latter indicates the amount of land at one hundred varas for Severino, as for nearly all of the recipients. For the expansion of Hispanic settlement in the Taos Valley, see Frank, "From Settler to Citizen," 200.

36. Bowden, "Private Land Claims," 4:930-31, n. 5.

37. Minge, "Last Will and Testament," 38.

38. Ibid., 55.

39. For further details about this San Cristóbal grant, which came to involve other claimants and whose story I have simplified, see Bowden, "Private Land Claims," 4:915–19, and below, chapter 7.

40. Minge, "Last Will and Testament," 39—and see the dispersals from the estate for amounts of corn and wheat. "The people are all more or less farmers, but generally on a small scale. Some more wealthy are able to carry on to advantage; the only grain raised is Corn and Wheat, which at this time is worth 4 dollars an *aneagre* [a *fanega*], (say 1 1/2" bushels) peas, beans, and pumpkins are also raised, bearing a price similar to the other." Wilson McGunnegle, letter from "San Francisco del Rancho (Taus) [*sic*], Province of New Mexico," June 30, 1823, St. Louis *Missouri Republican*, September 3, 1823; this reference is courtesy of Janet Lecompte.

41. John O. Baxter, *Las Carneradas: Sheep Trade in New Mexico, 1700–1860* (Albuquerque: University of New Mexico Press, 1987), 42, 90.

42. Ibid., 20; and Marc E. Simmons, *Albuquerque: A Narrative History* (Albuquerque: University of New Mexico Press, 1982), 114.

43. Minge, "Last Will and Testament," 38, 46. Martínez thought he had about one thousand sheep; his heirs counted 1,152 on August 2, 1827. As Minge indicates (p. 46), the will also gives the figure of 1,552 sheep and goats, but a tally of the distribution of animals that follows reveals that the figure is in error and should be a total of 1,212 sheep and goats.

44. José Agustín de Escudero's census, summarized in Baxter, *Las Carneradas*, 90. If these figures are roughly correct, don Severino had a larger percentage of horses and cattle relative to sheep and goats than most of his neighbors.

45. Weber, *The Mexican Frontier*, 212; and Baxter, *Las Carneradas*, 94–95.

46. Chávez, *But Time and Chance*, 18, citing baptismal book B–38, Taos.

47. Minge, "Last Will and Testament," 36.

48. See Martínez to Trujillo, Taos, [Sept.] 24, 1816, in the case of Martínez versus Francisco Sánchez, Taos, May 5–20, 1818, in SANM, roll 19, frames 105–25, discussed below in chapter 3.

49. Ramón A. Gutiérrez, *When Jesus Came, the Corn Mothers Went Away: Marriage, Sexuality, and Power in New Mexico, 1500–1846* (Stanford: Stanford University Press, 1991), 186–87.

50. The first quote is from Harvey Fergusson, *Río Grande* (1st ed., 1931; New York: Tudor Publishing, 1945), 81; the second is from Ruth G. Fish, "La Hacienda de Don Pascual Is Located on Río de Pueblo Near Taos," *The Taos Review* (June 1, 1940).

51. Martínez termed his family's rural holdings as, "*haciendas de campo, que se cuidaban lejos del poblado.*" [Martínez], *Historia cons[c]isa del cura de Taos.*

52. Fish, "La Hacienda de Don Pascual." Fish interviewed the widow of Severino's grandson, Agapito Martínez, doña Virginia Gonzáles de Martínez, "the last of the Martínez line to live in the house."

CHAPTER
❖ THREE

Markets, Mules, and Prosperity

By the early 1800s, as the Martínez family began to build a new life in Taos, New Mexico's economy had undergone deep structural changes. External markets, which hardly existed in don Severino's youth, had opened up and internal markets had expanded dramatically. A barter economy had begun to yield to the use of currency.[1] Hispanic Taos itself continued to grow rapidly. Between 1800 and 1810, the number of *vecinos* rose from 738 to 1,267, *vecinos* being an all-encompassing category of "Spaniards and people of all classes" that excluded Pueblo Indians.[2]

Markets

As at Abiquiú, Martínez had ample opportunities in Taos to trade with Indians. The Taos Valley had long been the scene of New Mexico's liveliest trade fairs with Plains peoples. Although those annual autumn fairs had ended in the mid-1780s, Spaniards continued to trade with the so-called pagan Indians,[3] exchanging horses; agricultural products, including sugar, tobacco, corn, bread, and dried fruit; and manufactured goods, such as hatchets, war axes, lances, knives, scissors, mirrors, and cloth for "Indian captives of both sexes, mules, moccasins, colts, mustangs, all kinds of hides and buffalo meat." So Gov. Fernando de Chacón observed in 1803, and, he added, "the balance of the trade always comes out in favor of the Spaniards."[4]

From his earliest years in the village of Taos, Martínez had opportunities for illegal trade with Americans. Itinerant Anglo-American merchants, peddling manufactured goods for the Indian trade, hovered on the periphery of New Mexico after the United States acquired the Louisiana country in 1803. Spain generally prohibited foreigners from trading in the closed economy of its empire, but some American merchants tried nonetheless to sell their wares in New Mexico. Baptiste La Lande, for example, a French-American who crossed the Plains from Illinois to New Mexico in 1804 with some $2,000 worth of merchandise, never took his profits home. Following arrest and detention in Chihuahua, La Lande returned to New Mexico and settled in Taos, where Severino Martínez and his neighbors knew him as Juan Bautista Lalanda.[5]

Other trappers and traders from the United States passed through Taos in La Lande's wake. Although some ran afoul of Mexican authorities, others probably traded successfully and left without a trace in the historical record. They offered high-quality manufactured goods at lower prices than New Mexicans could obtain through legal channels, especially after 1810, when a decade of little rebellions in Mexico disrupted the normal channels of trade.[6]

For Severino Martínez and other New Mexicans, the only legal external markets lay far to the south, over the long trail that followed the Río Grande to El Paso, 330 miles south of Santa Fe. From there, some traders continued nearly another three hundred miles to Chihuahua and beyond that to points even farther south. Others traveled west from El Paso to Sonora (where they reportedly had access to contraband from English merchants) or east into Coahuila.[7]

During Martínez's lifetime, tax incentives and government initiatives had helped to stimulate New Mexico's commerce and the quality of its locally made products, what New Mexicans called "*efectos del país.*"[8] Meanwhile, an invigorated mining economy throughout northern New Spain had increased demand for products from New Mexico. New Mexico itself lacked rich mines, but every November a convoy of New Mexicans with a military escort left New Mexico, driving large herds of sheep and pack mules laden with woolen textiles, cotton, hides, and piñón nuts. By 1806 trade had increased so dramatically that the mule trains traveled south twice a year, in spring and fall, although most traders preferred to depart in August because by then summer rains had filled water holes along the way.[9] Severino Martínez may have sent some of the production of his own hacienda on consignment with other merchants. We know, however, that he himself made this journey on at least one occasion, in 1816, when he traded in Sonora.[10]

When New Mexican merchants of Martínez's day returned home to their waiting families from Chihuahua and other points south, they brought horses, mules, various kinds of cloth, chocolate, sugar loaves, soap, rice, iron, hardware, spices, hats, leather goods, paper, drugs, and hard cash.[11] These imports, together with some locally made products, allowed New Mexican traders to offer a variety of merchandise to their customers. For example, an inventory of the stock in Manuel Delgado's store in Santa Fe in 1815 listed:

> *wool carders, looms, spindles, needlework and "counter" scissors, needles and firecrackers, razors and hair combs, mirrors and buttons and rosaries, ribbon, vermilion in packages, cigarette papers and mouth organs, coffee pots, 14 packages of face powder and 16 pounds of chocolate, four packages of saffron and 21 sacks of rice, 48 pounds of sugar, 5 pounds of copper sulphate, miscellaneous steel, iron and copper, candlesticks, 260 quarts of whiskey, olive oil, pots and pans, washbowls from Michoacán, 41 chairs and small stools, flour, corn, chile, carpets, knives (one to cut cheese with), and 53 cups and dishes from Puebla, Mexico.*[12]

Late in the colonial period, then, but well before trade with Anglo Americans became legalized in 1821, affluent New Mexicans like the Martínez family had access to a variety of manufactured goods.[13] They also enjoyed a market, although a distant one, for products they obtained in trade from Indians and products they raised or manufactured. When he died in 1827 Severino Martínez's estate included items that suggest his involvement in both the Indian trade and the Chihuahua trade. He owned sheep, locally made textiles, and hides—all mainstays of trade with Chihuahua—in quantities that exceeded the needs of his family.[14] Among his livestock, his heirs counted more than fifteen hundred sheep on his lands.[15] Don Severino may have marketed those sheep on the hoof in Chihuahua, but the modest size of his flocks, and the additional distance he had to drive the animals, probably put him at a disadvantage in competition with sheep raisers in the Río Abajo. More likely, don Severino marketed products made from wool (its bulk in relation to its value made the shipment of raw wool uneconomical). Severino's will included forty-four pairs of wool stockings and twenty-nine varas of a woolen sheeting (*sabanilla*)—commonplaces of the Chihuahua trade.[16] Textiles, apparently of local manufacture, included 120 varas of cotton blanket (*manta*), destined perhaps for markets to the south.[17] Finally, his possessions included 124 buffalo hides and twenty-five deerskins, items that New Mexicans had traditionally obtained through the Indian trade and marketed in the south.[18]

Direct documentary evidence of don Severino's personal involvement in either the Indian trade or the Chihuahua trade, however, is limited to a single episode in 1818, which landed him in jail and resulted in a judicial investigation.

The alcalde and the mule

On May 5, 1818, on his third day in a jail cell, his legs clamped in stocks, Severino Martínez wrote to New Mexico's governor, Pedro María de Allande, appealing to him for justice. The alcalde of Taos, Martínez charged, had put him in jail without just cause. Three days before, on the morning of May 3, after the congregation had left Mass, Alcalde Juan de Dios Peña had put him in stocks secured by ropes and ordered two Indians to guard him and to prevent anyone from communicating with him. Then, to further shame and embarrass him, the alcalde had organized an Indian dance at three in the afternoon in front of his cell so that everyone "might see the state I was in." After the passage of three days, the alcalde still would not loosen the stocks, "even though he knows that I lack use of my legs and that I am falling behind in my household tasks."[19]

Not surprisingly, the alcalde of Taos saw the episode somewhat differently. Alcalde Juan de Dios Peña explained to the governor that the trouble had begun earlier, on April 25, when Martínez had requested that the alcalde resolve a long-standing dispute Martínez had with the Sánchez family over a mule. The alcalde explained that he would have to write to the alcalde of La Cañada, in whose jurisdiction the Sánchez family lived, to obtain declarations from the other side in the case. Martínez became abusive at this point, accusing Peña of favoring the Sánchez family, refusing to listen to reason, and repeatedly accusing the alcalde of bias.

A week later, Martínez visited Alcalde Peña again, asking him for the proceedings in the case of the disputed mule so that he could send them to the governor for resolution. Peña refused and Martínez insulted him again, calling him a blind, prejudiced judge. Peña demanded in the name of the king that

Martínez stop insulting him and threatened him with jail. As Martínez started to leave, Peña gave him a push that sent don Severino flying down a staircase. Martínez then fled without acknowledging Peña's authority.

Peña, a retired military officer, would not tolerate Martínez's arrogance. He arrested the still-abusive Martínez and put him in stocks but denied that he held Martínez incommunicado. To the contrary. Shortly after he put Martínez in jail, Father José Benito Pereyro came by with a servant to bring Martínez chocolate; after lunch the priest returned with a drink; in the afternoon the priest stopped in to amuse Martínez with a deck of cards. As to the charge that he arranged an Indian dance in order to embarrass Martínez, the alcalde explained that Indians danced in the plaza on every feast day and that May 3 was the day of the Holy Cross.

Peña angrily dismissed Martínez's accusation that he had thrown him in jail without cause. Don Severino, the alcalde said, was "so hard-headed, so self-absorbed that he would not recognize the truth even if it were shoved in front of his eyes." Moreover, he linked Martínez to the insurgencies that had swept Mexico sporadically since 1810: "Any man who raises his voice in such a disorderly way in public against a judge shows signs it seems to me of wanting to declare a Republic and make himself its ringleader." Peña, then, portrayed Martínez as a traitor as well as a shameless liar who lacked respect for the law and its representatives. Martínez would stay in the stocks, Peña said, until the governor decided what to do with him.[20]

On May 13, Governor Allande sent to Taos his personal representative, the alcalde of the district of Santa Cruz de la Cañada, Matías Ortiz. The governor ordered Ortiz to investigate two matters. First, to see why Peña held Martínez prisoner. Had don Severino insulted the alcalde without reason? Had the alcalde performed his duties properly? Second, Matías Ortiz was to get to the bottom of the dispute over the mule, which had caused the disturbance in the first place. The governor ordered Ortiz to leave without delay.[21]

Matías Ortiz lost no time. Arriving in Taos on May 16 he found Severino Martínez with his legs still in stocks but now contrite. Martínez acknowledged his errors and asked that he be pardoned for his failings "for the love of God." Then, in a remarkable about-face, Alcalde Peña raised Martínez in his arms, pardoned him, and dropped the charges, saying that Martínez had suffered punishment enough.[22]

The dispute over the mule, however, remained unsettled. On May 18 and 19, Matías Ortiz took testimony from seven participants or witnesses. The case had its origins nearly two years earlier, in the late summer of 1816, when Pedro Antonio Lucero and Vicente Trujillo had traveled from Taos in a party headed to the country of "Indian allies" to trade. Along the way, Lucero loaned Trujillo a light brown he-mule that he could use "to buy an Indian." The group apparently followed a well-worn trail up the Río Grande into the San Luis Valley in today's southern Colorado, then made its way over Sangre de Cristo Pass to the edge of the High Plains. They got at least as far as Huerfano Creek, a tributary of the Arkansas River in today's southeastern Colorado. Somewhere in this country Trujillo gave the brown he-mule, along with another, to Indians the Spaniards called "big ears"—"*orejones*"—in exchange for an Indian girl—an "*indita*."[23] On this much all could agree.

Disagreement arose over whose mule Lucero had loaned to Trujillo. Lucero apparently believed that the mule belonged to Francisco Sánchez. Sánchez had told Lucero that the mule was on the Río Latir (a tributary of the Costilla Creek, more than thirty miles north of Taos) and that he could take the mule if he could find it.[24] Lucero found a mule and took it, but some of his companions believed he had taken the wrong mule, one belonging to Severino Martínez.

Vicente Trujillo could not be sure whose mule he had traded for the Indian girl. Upon returning from the Indian country, Trujillo wrote a courteous note to Martínez, paying respect to his "illustrious family." Trujillo explained to don Severino that Pedro Lucero had loaned him a light brown mule that he might trade. Some said the mule belonged to Francisco Sánchez but others identified it as the property of don Severino. If Martínez was missing a mule of this color, he should come by and choose one of Trujillo's eight mules as recompense.[25]

Don Severino responded to Trujillo in writing, beginning with customary courtesy and expressing pleasure at Trujillo's safe return before getting to the point. The mule belonged to him. Martínez had searched for it on the Río Latir, wasting considerable time and losing work. Another mule would not compensate him. For his trouble, Martínez wanted the Indian girl, and to sweeten the deal he would give Trujillo a she-mule and two he-mules.[26] When Trujillo declined to accept those terms, Martínez appealed to the alcalde of Taos and to the governor for justice, later explaining that he had purchased the mule in March 1816 in Sonora.[27]

Meanwhile, the Sánchez family insisted that the mule that Trujillo traded for the Indian girl belonged to them. Francisco Sánchez died while the case dragged on, but his nephews took up his cause. In September 1817, a year after the episode, Miguel Sánchez argued that the mule Trujillo had traded belonged to his uncle, Francisco. The mule bore the family's brand, he said, and he named several people who could identify it.[28] The following year, in May 1818, another nephew of Francisco Sánchez and the executor of his estate, Antonio Sánchez, also testified that the brown mule carried the Sánchez brand.[29]

On May 20, 1818, his investigation completed, Matías Ortiz gathered together all of the papers in the suit and sent them to the governor to render the final judgment. The evidence as Ortiz presented it favored Martínez.[30] Don Severino's intemperate outbursts against Alcalde Juan de Dios Peña had landed him in jail, but his contrition and determination apparently carried the day.

As with most frontiersmen, Martínez left little trace of his daily activities in the written records. These exceptional hearings in the case of the brown mule, and Martínez's bitter exchange with the alcalde of Taos, offer a rare glimpse into Martínez's determined and passionate character. The hearings also offer a view into the world he inhabited, where a mule purchased in Sonora would go toward the price of an Indian girl in northern New Mexico and where no one honored the well-known laws against buying, selling, owning, or enslaving Indians.[31]

Don Severino's verbal assault on the alcalde of Taos is ironic in that Martínez himself became alcalde of Taos on at least two occasions, in 1821 and 1825, and was himself the target of insults by an unhappy petitioner in 1825. One Juan de Jesús Vigil, bitter over a ruling, spread rumors from Taos to Santa Fe that his case "demonstrated the despotic, false, and unjust manner" of Alcalde Martínez. Don Severino's oldest son, Padre Antonio José, wrote to the governor himself, lashing out against Vigil and demanding vindication of his family's honor.[32]

Affluence

By the 1810s, if not before, Severino Martínez, known to his neighbors as "don," had become patriarch of "perhaps the most affluent family in Taos" in the judgment of one historian.[33] Affluence is, of course, a relative condition. Although trade had increased and the New Mexican economy had boomed, visitors still found the arid province remote and impoverished. New Mexico, lamented Gov. Alberto Máynez in 1815, "does not have the resources to prosper; it is a country impoverished by nature."[34] "The people are generally poor, having neither industry nor commerce," a visitor from the United States observed in 1818.[35] "Never," wrote one cleric from Durango who traveled to New Mexico in 1817 and 1818, "have I visited a more unfortunate place, unexceeded in the scarcity and poverty of its residents who are unable to supply themselves." The isolated New Mexicans, he said, "have to live without hope of any help, agitated continuously by war."36

By war, the cleric from Durango meant raids by nomadic or seminomadic Indians on the *vecinos* and the Pueblo Indians. In the last years of Spanish rule, tensions between New Mexicans and neighboring tribes had mounted as things fell apart.

NOTES

1. See chapter 1, and Ross Frank, "From Settler to Citizen: Economic Development and Cultural Change in Late Colonial New Mexico, 1750–1820" (Ph.D. diss., University of California, Berkeley, 1992), 231–47, and Martha A. Works, "Trade and the Emergence of Global Culture in Spanish Colonial New Mexico," in Kent Mathewson, ed., *Culture, Form, and Place: Essays in Cultural and Historical Geography, Geoscience, and Man* (Baton Rouge: Dept. of Geography and Anthropology, 1993), 157–93.

2. Frank, "From Settler to Citizen," 418, 420; "Españoles y gente de todas clases." Census of Fr. José Benito Pereyro, Santa Fe, December 31, 1810, Ritch Papers, no. 68, Huntington Library, San Marino, California.

3. Charles L. Kenner, *A History of New Mexican–Plains Indian Relations* (Norman: University of Oklahoma Press, 1969), 36–40, 44, 46, 64. Marc Simmons, *Spanish Government in New Mexico* (Albuquerque: University of New Mexico Press, 1968), 185, suggests that Taos had the liveliest fairs.

4. Marc Simmons, ed. and trans., "The Chacón Economic Report of 1803," *NMHR* 60 (January 1985):87.

5. David J. Weber, *The Taos Trappers: The Fur Trade in the Far Southwest, 1540–1846* (Norman: University of Oklahoma Press, 1971), 36–37. For a summary of efforts by foreigners to trade in New Mexico, see ibid., chapter 2.

6. Weber, *Taos Trappers*, 37–50.

7. On the English contraband, see Alfred B. Thomas, ed. and trans., "An Anonymous Description of New Mexico, 1818," *Southwestern Historical Quarterly* 33 (July 1929):58.

8. Ward Alan Minge, "Efectos del País: A History of Weaving along the Río Grande," in *Spanish Textile Tradition of New Mexico and Colorado* (Santa Fe: Museum of New Mexico Press, 1979), 8–28, has a fine discussion of this topic.

9. Frank, "From Settler to Citizen," 247–49; and John O. Baxter to Weber, Santa Fe, August 29, 1994.

10. The story is noted below in this chapter.

11. Simmons, "Chacón Economic Report," 86.

12. A summary of this part of Delgado's will by David H. Snow, "'Purchased in Chihuahua for Feasts,'" in Gabrielle G. Palmer, comp., *El Camino Real de Tierra Adentro* (Santa Fe: Bureau of Land Management, 1993), 142. See, too, Minge, "Efectos del País," 24.

13. Jeffrey L. Boyer, "La Puente: Eighteenth-Century Hispanic Village Life on the Río Chama Frontier," in Bradley J. Vierra and Clara Gualtieri, eds., *Current Research on the Late Prehistory and Early History of New Mexico* (Albuquerque: New Mexico Archaeological Council Special Publication 1, July 1992), 234, argues that in the Spanish Colonial era "items of nonlocal production were relatively rare . . . particularly in isolated frontier settings." The well-to-do, however, possessed some rather exotic imports even on a remote ranch near Abiquiú, as is clear in Richard Eighme Ahlborn, "The Will of a Woman in 1762," *NMHR* 65 (July 1990):319–55.

14. Frank, "From Settler to Citizen," 247–64, discusses these exports.

15. Martínez thought he had a thousand sheep; the count came to 1,555. Ward Alan Minge, ed. and trans., "The Last Will and Testament of Don Severino Martínez," *New Mexico Quarterly* 33 (Spring 1963):38 and 46.

16. Ibid., 39, 44–46.

17. Ibid., 45–46. His wife received sixty varas and the children the other sixty between them. The will also identified 160 varas of linen (p. 39), but that might have been of American manufacture.

18. Minge, "Last Will and Testament," 39.

19. Martínez to Governor Allande, May 5, 1818, in the case of Martínez versus Francisco Sánchez, Taos, May 5–20, 1818, in SANM, roll 19, frames 105–25. References that follow derive from this case; I am grateful to my former student, Jennifer Keen, who made the initial transcriptions of these documents.

20. Peña to Allande, May 10, 1818.

21. Allande to Ortiz, May 13, 1818.

22. Statement of Matías Ortiz, May 16, 1818.

23. Testimonies of Pedro Lucero and Vicente Trujillo, May 18, 1818.

24. Miguel Sánchez to the alcalde of Taos, San Gerónimo de Taos, September 8, 1817, and testimony of Antonio Sánchez, nephew and executor of the estate of the deceased Francisco Sánchez, Taos, May 19, 1818. Antonio Sánchez refers to the mule on the Río Datil, but he was probably mistaken; all other testimony points to the Latir.

25. Trujillo to Martínez, Taos, September 24, 1816.

26. Martínez to Trujillo, Taos, [September] 24, 1816.

27. Testimony of Severino Martínez, San Gerónimo de Taos, May 19, 1818.

28. Miguel Sánchez to the alcalde of Taos, San Gerónimo de Taos, September 8, 1817.

29. Testimony of Antonio Sánchez, San Gerónimo de Taos, May 19, 1818.

30. Ortiz called the governor's attention to the fact that Antonio Sánchez testified that his uncle, Francisco, had purchased his missing mule from Juan Andrés de Archuleta and that the mule had Archuleta's brand. Trujillo, however, denied that the mule he traded for the Indian girl carried Archuleta's brand. Thus, Ortiz told the governor, the mule that Trujillo traded could not have belonged to the Sánchez family.

31. See, for example, the comandante general, July 17, 1812, to the governor of New Mexico, pointing to a law in the *Recopilacion de Indias* (libro VI, título II, ley 1.a) "that Indians are free and not subject to servitude." The governor distributed a copy of that document to alcaldes in New Mexico, including Taos, where Alcalde Tomás Ortiz acknowledged receipt and promised obedience, in SANM, roll 17, frames 554–56.

32. Antonio José Martínez to Gov. Antonio Narbona, Taos, December 12, 1825, in MANM, roll 4, frames 764–67. For more on Martínez as alcalde, see below.

33. Angélico Chávez, *But Time and Chance: The Story of Padre Martínez of Taos, 1793–1867* (Santa Fe: Sunstone Press, 1981), 18.

34. Governor Máynez to Bernardo Bonavia, Santa Fe, September 18, 1815, in SANM, roll 18, frames 243–45, called to my attention by Janet Lecompte. See, too, Marc Simmons, "Misery as a Factor in New Mexican Colonial Life," *Reflections: Papers on Southwestern Culture History in Honor of Charles H. Lange. Papers of the Archaeological Society of New Mexico*, vol. 14, Anne V. Poore, ed. (Santa Fe: Ancient City Press, 1988), 227–30.

35. Thomas, "Anonymous Description," 58.

36. Report of Juan Bautista Ladrón del Niño de Guevara to Juan Francisco de Castañiza, Bishop of Durango, Durango, October 23, 1820 (based on visits to New Mexico in 1817 and 1818), in AASF, roll 45, frames 285–302.

CHAPTER
❖ FOUR

Twilight of Empire

At ten o'clock at night, on September 10, 1821, a band of Comanches rode into the plaza of Taos, menacing the town as they had not done in recent memory. They circled the plaza, seized three boys, and insulted the citizenry. Holding the boys hostage, the Comanches killed some goats, stole roosters and hens, and then rode out of town. They released the boys unharmed, but before they rode away they circled the edges of town as if assessing its manpower and strength.

The episode terrified the *vecinos*. They feared the Comanches would return to pillage their homes at a time when they lacked manpower to defend themselves. Many residents had already left the Taos Valley due to "calamities" and shortages of food. To make matters worse, Gov. Facundo Melgares had called on able-bodied men to join an autumn campaign against the Navajos. The town council of Taos asked Governor Melgares to excuse the *vecinos* of Taos from military service, lest the Taos Valley stand exposed to attack from Comanches. If he did not accede to their request, the councilmen threatened, residents of the valley would move their families to another district to keep them from harm's way. The Taos Valley "would remain deserted."[1]

Governor Melgares might have regarded the town council's claim that it feared a Comanche attack on Taos with some suspicion, for the *vecinos* had much to lose and little to gain on a military campaign against Navajos. They had to supply their own rations, weapons, ammunition, and mounts, and they received no pay.[2] Still, Melgares apparently had reason to believe the story was genuine for he granted the request.[3]

Even allowing for exaggerations by the town council, or *ayuntamiento*, of Taos, the Taos Valley had become more dangerous and impoverished. First, its *vecino* population had lost ground. The number of Hispanic residents had declined from 1,353 in 1811 to 1,260 at the end of 1821.[4] Through natural increase alone, the population should have grown, so it seems likely that some of the *vecinos* abandoned the valley as the *ayuntamiento* of Taos had claimed. Second, Taos suffered from a temporary food shortage. The American trapper Jacob Fowler, who passed through Taos later that winter, noted in his journal (with his characteristic phonetic spelling and eccentric punctuation):

We Heare found the people extremely poor. and Bread Stuff Coud not be Head amongst them as the[y] Said the grass hopers Head Eat up all their grain for the last two years. . . . We found them Eaqually Scarce of meet [meat]. . . . We must Soon leave this Reeched [wretched] place.[5]

Third, relations between Hispanos and nomads, tense and tenuous in the best of circumstances, had deteriorated in the waning years of Spanish control.

Following Napoleon's invasion of the Iberian peninsula in 1808, Spain's American colonies had begun to rebel. The crisis interrupted everyday life even in areas as remote and loyal to the empire as New Mexico. There, trade was disrupted, supplies for the military and the missions became erratic, and soldiers and officials often went unpaid. At the same time, carefully wrought treaties with Apaches, Comanches, Navajos, and other autonomous and potentially hostile Indians began to unravel because frontiersmen could no longer command sufficient military respect or deliver agreed-upon gifts.[6]

New Mexicans in the smallest of communities felt the impact of the shortages. Pablo Lucero of Taos, for example, had to entertain a party of Kiowas at his house for four days in July 1815. In the past he would have been reimbursed from a special fund for his expenses, which included butchering a "fat cow" for the Kiowas. Now, however, the governor could find no money in that special fund—the *fondo de aliados*.7

In the past, generous gifts helped to compensate Indians for outrages committed by individual Spaniards. Without gifts, those outrages could incite Indians to revenge, as in the early summer of 1818 when four *vecinos* from Taos killed, "without any cause," a Jicarilla Apache man, two women, and a small boy.8

Facundo Melgares, who assumed the governorship in 1818, understood one solution to the problem. He needed to apply more force against the "heathen" because "lacking the gifts to which they are accustomed, they begin to threaten the province."9 To meet the pressing need for ammunition, he asked that the bell of the military chapel in Santa Fe, together with other ironwork, be melted down to make shot; his request was granted.10

"Barbaric" indians and anglo americans

Severino Martínez, like many New Mexicans, had prospered with the expansion of markets and the greater circulation of hard cash after the mid-1780s. The boom had ended by 1815, if not before, and the Martínez family fortunes probably declined in the last years of Spanish rule as tensions and insecurities rose. Residents of Taos not only worried about growing Indian hostilities, they feared an invasion from the neighboring United States as well. In their worst nightmares, New Mexican officials imagined that Anglo Americans would seize the province with the aid of "barbaric, heathen, and hostile" Indians.11

Taos, "the last mission" situated on the edge of "heathen" lands, seemed especially vulnerable.12 No garrison normally protected it or the passes leading to it. Tensions at Taos rose and fell depending on the rumor of the moment, reaching a crescendo in the late summer of 1818. Then one José Cayetano Hernández, who claimed to have fled from Pawnee captivity, arrived in Taos bearing news that a group of Anglo Americans and Pawnees planned to invade New Mexico when "the leaves fell from the poplars." Governor Melgares mobilized hundreds of men, including militia, to locate the invaders and defend the province. One scouting party, led by "don José Antonio Martínez" of Taos—perhaps a relative of don Severino's—reconnoitered the San Luis and Arkansas valleys of today's southern Colorado and then continued up the Front Range of the Rockies to Manitou Springs, where Hernández said the invaders planned to rendezvous.13

They returned without encountering invaders, but the fear remained. Anglo Americans had already taken advantage of Spain's weaknesses to seize territory in Florida, to invade Texas, and to press claims that Louisiana extended well into Spanish territory. As far away as Madrid, Spanish officials knew that Anglo Americans had reconnoitered New Mexico and had determined its vulnerability through undefended routes from the Great Plains, including Taos Pass.[14]

A PRIEST IN THE FAMILY

However tense or difficult the last years of Spanish rule might have been for New Mexicans, Severino Martínez still possessed sufficient resources to support the long seminary education of one of his children. In 1817 Antonio José entered a seminary in Durango; six years later he returned to New Mexico as a priest.

This was a remarkable achievement in New Mexico of that era, one that neither Severino nor María del Carmel could have anticipated for their eldest son. In two centuries only one New Mexican had become a priest—and that isolated case had occurred beyond living memory.[15] One reason was plain. New Mexico had only rudimentary schools and no seminary, so its young men had to leave the province to study and that required financial support beyond the means of most *vecinos*, even those who studied on a scholarship, as did Antonio José. Some years later Severino noted in his will that Antonio José owed him 891 pesos "for expenses and costs in his literary career"—a reference to his seminary training.[16]

Antonio José had seemed an unlikely candidate for the priesthood. As was the custom of the day, don Severino had arranged for his son's marriage, at age nineteen, to María de la Luz Martín of Abiquiú. The wedding took place in Abiquiú on May 20, 1812, in a double ceremony where Severino had also arranged for his younger daughter, twelve-year-old Juana María, to marry the brother of María de la Luz Martín—Antonio José's betrothed (at the end of his life, Severino took pride in the fact that he had "placed in the estate of matrimony" all but one of his children).[17]

Antonio José and his new bride apparently made their home in Abiquiú until tragedy struck. Fourteen months after the wedding, María de la Luz died in childbirth.[18] The widowed Antonio José returned to his parents' house. His infant daughter, also named María de la Luz, seems to have stayed with her mother's family at Abiquiú.[19]

Antonio José did not remarry but worked on his family's hacienda. There he cultivated a portion of the land that was his by raising small animals, and he contributed to his parents' income.[20] Four years after his wife's death, early in

1817, he traveled south through Santa Fe, El Paso, and Chihuahua to Durango, where at age twenty-four he entered the Seminario Tridentino de Durango on a scholarship.[21] Perhaps don Severino had made contact with the seminary earlier while on a trading venture to the south.

Antonio José remained at the seminary in Durango for nearly six years. In January 1823, suffering from what he described as a "palpitation that impaired . . . breathing," he left Durango as an ordained priest—a *presbítero*, or *cura*—and returned to his parents' home in Taos.[22] Severino and María probably went to the chapel of Nuestra Señora de Guadalupe to hear him preach his first sermon in Taos on April 20, 1823, within a week of his return. In that sermon he expressed gratitude for the prayers of his neighbors and his characteristic loyalty and affection for his community:

> *When I found myself fatigued in my laborious tasks, surrounded by my scholastic labors, and in many other troubles, . . . I offered up my supplications to our God, and put my mind on this our homeland. I would reflect on the necessities under which you were laboring, and would feel a resolute spirit and intention to continue.*[23]

In the few years remaining to them, Severino and María Martínez would have more opportunities to take pride in their son, for he had come home at a propitious moment to advance his career as a priest. He had left for the seminary in Durango when New Mexico still belonged to Spain; when he returned, it had become part of an independent Mexico.

Notes

1. Pedro Martín to Alcalde Pablo Lucero, Taos, September 12, 1821, and Pablo Lucero and the *ayuntamiento* of Taos to the governor, Taos, September 13, 1821, in SANM, roll 20, frames 769–70. The reference is courtesy of Janet Lecompte.

2. Report of Juan Bautista Ladrón del Niño de Guevara to Juan Francisco de Castañiza, Bishop of Durango, Durango, October 23, 1820 (based on visits to New Mexico of 1817 and 1818), in AASF, roll 45, frames 285–302; and David J. Weber, *The Mexican Frontier, 1821–1846: The American Southwest under Mexico* (Albuquerque: University of New Mexico Press, 1982), 117, citing another contemporary account of 1828.

3. A rough draft of Governor Melgares's reply appears on the petition of the *ayuntamiento* of Taos to the governor, Taos, September 13, 1821, cited in n. 1.

4. Ross Frank, "From Settler to Citizen: Economic Development and Cultural Change in Late Colonial New Mexico, 1750–1820" (Ph.D. diss.,

University of California, Berkeley, 1992): 420, 421, 423.

5. Elliott Coues, ed., *The Journal of Jacob Fowler*, with additional notes by Raymund W. and Mary Lund Settle and Harry R. Stevens (Lincoln: University of Nebraska Press, 1970), 90–91.

6. Weber, *The Mexican Frontier*, 11.

7. Pablo Lucero to Gov. Alberto Máynez, Taos, August 16, 1815, and Máynez's reply, [Santa Fe,] August 20, 1815, in SANM, roll 18, frames 137–38.

8. Pedro María de Allande to the alcaldes of Cañada, Abiquiú, and Taos, Santa Fe, July 1, 1818, in SANM, roll 19, frames 153–54.

9. Fragment of a draft of a letter from Facundo Melgares to an unknown party, Santa Fe, August 25, 1821, in SANM, roll 20, frames 740–41.

10. Arthur Gómez, "Royalist in Transition: Facundo Melgares, the Last Spanish Governor of New Mexico, 1818–1822," *NMHR* 68 (October 1993):380. Ladrón del Niño de Guevara to Castañiza, October 23, 1820.

11. Ladrón del Niño de Guevara to Castañiza, October 23, 1820.

12. Ibid.

13. A. B. Thomas, "Documents Bearing Upon the Northern Frontier of New Mexico, 1818–1819," *NMHR* 4 (April 1929):152, 158, and 159.

14. Alfred B. Thomas, ed. and trans., "An Anonymous Description of New Mexico, 1818," *Southwestern Historical Quarterly* 33 (July 1929):50-74. For an overview of Spanish reactions to perceived Anglo-American aggression toward New Mexico and guidance to sources, see Gómez, "Royalist in Transition," 371–87.

15. Angélico Chávez, *But Time and Chance: The Story of Padre Martínez of Taos, 1793–1867* (Santa Fe: Sunstone Press, 1981), 20, who points to Santiago Roybal as the single exception.

16. Ward Alan Minge, ed. and trans., "The Last Will and Testament of Don Severino Martínez," *New Mexico Quarterly* 33 (Spring 1963):37.

17. Minge, "Last Will and Testament," 40; and Chávez, *But Time and Chance*, 18.

18. Chávez, *But Time and Chance*, 18–19.

19. On this last point, see ibid., 24–25.

20. Severino Martínez referred to those years in his will. Minge, "Last Will and Testament," 37.

21. Antonio José Martínez, *Relación de Méritos del Presbítero Antonio José Martínez . . . cura engargado de Taos en el Departamento de Nuevo Mexico* (Taos: Impresa de su oficina á cargo de Jesus Maria Baca, 1838), 3. Cecil V. Romero, ed. and trans., "Apologia of Presbyter Antonio J. Martínez . . . 1838," *NMHR* 3 (October 1928):329.

22. "[S]é enfermó de cierto latido que le embarasaba la respiracion." Martínez, *Relación de Méritos*, 17; and Romero, "Apologia," 336.

23. The sermon is reproduced in full in Santiago Valdez, "Biography of Padre Antonio José Martínez, cura-pastor of Parish of Taos, N.Mex., A.D. 1877," by Santiago Valdez, Rev. Juan Romero, trans. (unpublished manuscript, 1993), 12–16; quote is on p. 15.

CHAPTER
❖ FIVE

inds

OF CHANGE:

A MEXICAN

TERRITORY

IN APRIL 1821, New Mexican officials learned from Gov. Facundo Melgares that a Spanish officer, Agustín de Iturbide, had declared Mexico's independence from Spain that winter. New Mexicans did not rush imprudently to join Iturbide's cause.[1] Following news of Iturbide's rebellion came an order from the viceroy, exhorting New Mexicans to remain loyal subjects of Ferdinand VII and condemning the "ungrateful" Iturbide and his "subversive plans." In customary fashion, Governor Melgares circulated copies of the viceroy's orders to alcaldes throughout New Mexico. Serving that year as alcalde of Taos, Severino Martínez signed the document and posted a copy in his district, or *alcaldía*. A communication from the governing council of Mexico City accompanied the viceroy's order; it expressed support for the viceroy and urged *vecinos* to renew their loyalty to the monarchy. Don Severino dutifully signed and proclaimed that document as well.[2]

New Mexico remained loyal to the Spanish Crown for a few more months until Governor Melgares's superior officer switched sides in recognition of the likelihood of Iturbide's triumph. Melgares followed suit. On September 11, 1821, Governor Melgares ordered officials in Santa Fe to take an oath of allegiance to Iturbide's government. The governor also sent dispatches to all alcaldes in New Mexico, ordering them to administer the same oath in their districts. Together with his fellow magistrates, Severino Martínez apparently carried out his instructions without protest. In this fashion, independence from Spain came to Taos, as it did to all of New Mexico. Unlike their compatriots in many other parts of Mexico, New Mexicans had the good fortune to gain independence without bloodshed.[3]

The extent to which individual New Mexicans welcomed or deplored the end of Spanish rule we may never know. It is clear, however, that independence brought enormous changes, as Mexico headed in new political, economic, and social directions; the winds of change altered the lives of individuals throughout the nation, even on its remote frontiers.

Don Severino in territorial politics

The new political course took Mexico through a brief experiment with monarchy under its liberator Agustín de Iturbide. Then in 1824, following the collapse of the monarchy, Mexico re-formed itself into the United States of Mexico, a constitutional republic, made up of states and territories resembling those of the United States. Too sparsely populated to form a state, New Mexico became a territory, headed by a governor advised by a seven-member territorial assembly, or *diputación*.[4]

Severino Martínez served for a year in the first *diputación* elected under Mexico's 1824 constitution. In March 1825, an electoral commission chose him as one of the seven assemblymen, or *vocales*,[5] and on July 16, 1825, he took the oath of office at the opening of the first session of the *diputación* in Santa Fe.[6]

Travel to the territorial capital—a round-trip of some 120 miles—must have represented a considerable inconvenience for don Severino, and the position offered no salary. Although he traveled at his own expense, only once during his term in the *diputación* did don Severino miss a meeting, an unusual single session held in mid-August.[7] Beginning with the first session of the fall, on

September 15, 1825, when the assembly welcomed a new governor, Antonio Narbona, and said farewells to the outgoing governor, Bartolomé Baca, through July of 1826, don Severino never missed a meeting. His regular attendance in Santa Fe seems especially remarkable because he concurrently served a one-year term as alcalde of Taos, as he had in 1821 and perhaps on other occasions as well.

The position of alcalde, which usually went to a member of the local oligarchy, entailed considerable responsibility.[8] As the chief magistrate of his town, an alcalde had judicial and legislative as well as executive duties, his responsibilities exceeding those of an Anglo-American mayor. An alcalde presided over meetings of the town council (a *cabildo* or *ayuntamiento*), heard minor legal cases, and administered the day-to-day operations of town government.[9] The job was burdensome enough that during don Severino's absence in Santa Fe, Taos needed an acting alcalde, a position filled by José Ignacio Córdova.[10]

Through his diligent participation in the *diputación* of 1825–26, Severino Martínez probably became more intimately acquainted with New Mexico's anomalous political position. Four years after Mexico declared independence, New Mexico was still governed by many laws of Spain. The constitution of 1824 required that Congress draw up regulations for the internal government of territories such as New Mexico, but Congress failed to do so until 1836. In the meantime, the Spanish Constitution of 1812 and certain laws of the liberal Spanish Cortes of Cádiz (1810–14) remained in force, so long as they did not conflict with Mexican laws. Martínez and his fellow assemblymen understood that perfectly. When, for example, one Simón Saenz of Taos asked for land at nearby Arroyo Hondo, the *diputación* ruled that the alcalde of Taos should make the grant and do so without collecting fees, as stipulated by a law "issued by the Spanish Cortes and in force up to the present date."[11]

In the absence of up-to-date regulations for the governance of territories, the *diputación* itself might have exercised considerable initiative, but its powers were exceedingly limited, hardly more than those of a consultative body. The assembly had responsibility for tax collection, missions, clerical abuses, and public health, public works, education, agriculture, industry, and commerce. It could not act without the approval of the central government or promulgate laws or decrees.

When Antonio José Martínez followed his father's example and served a term in the *diputación* in 1831, he complained formally to the Mexican Congress that the assembly needed greater authority. In practice, he said, the *diputación* concerned itself with only three functions: supervising primary schools, granting lands, and maintaining relations with Congress. It lacked authority to resolve the territory's most urgent problems: to carry out judicial and ecclesiastical reforms and defend the province against Indians. Why, he asked implicitly, should New Mexico's leaders lose time and money to serve in the assembly if they did not have power to effect significant reforms? Other New Mexico oligarchs shared Padre Martínez's dim view of the assembly's weakness and its need for authority to act.[12] Don Severino's attendance record suggests that he either believed that he filled some important function as an assemblyman or that he enjoyed the status of serving in Santa Fe.

Whatever the case, don Severino's term in the assembly probably taught him a good deal about the operations of the new republican government. Via the governor, the *diputación* received regular communications from New Mexico's representative in Congress, Santiago Abreú; from different ministers in Mexico City, including the secretary of state, the minister of justice and ecclesiastical affairs, and the minister of the treasury; and from the president himself, Guadalupe Victoria. Conversely, the New Mexican Assembly communicated with the central government through the governor.

Defense stood high on the assembly's agenda in 1825, as it had in the pre-republican era. As the assemblymen lamented in November of 1825, "besides being bounded by the United States, [New Mexico] has the inimitable circumstance of facing thirty-some tribes of savages who . . . threaten its ruin."[13] Congress, Santiago Abreú reported, planned to send four companies of cavalry to New Mexico but was not quite sure where to station the troops. The newly formed central government had so little information about New Mexico that it did not know its boundaries or the names of neighboring independent tribes.[14]

To advise the government about positioning the troops, the New Mexico Assembly appointed a two-man committee consisting of Rafael Sarracino and Severino Martínez. Officials had long looked to the Taos Valley as the site for a future garrison, and Martínez would certainly have welcomed one.[15] If New Mexico bordered on "tribes of savages," Taos was New Mexico's border. "The Indians in this neighborhood are very troublesome at times, and have but little hesitation in taking life for the sake of plunder," one American had reported from Taos in June 1823. "Five Americans," he added, "have been killed since June last, within sixty miles of this place."[16] Don Severino and his neighbors faced loss of property as well as life, as on March 11, 1826, when a group of Pawnees "entered the Valley & drove off in the Night a number of Mules & horses."[17]

Beyond questions of defense, membership in the assembly must have acquainted Martínez more fully with a variety of local concerns occasioned by the new regime. What would be the status and obligations of mission Indians in a republic? What of missions themselves, which the liberal Spanish Cortes at Cádiz had ordered to be secularized? How could the sacraments be delivered to Indian pueblos given the chronic shortage of priests? These matters were of vital concern to Severino's oldest son, Antonio José, then in search of a permanent parish; father and son must have discussed them.

The financing of public schools loomed large when Severino Martínez began his one-year term in the legislature. In the tradition of his time and place, don Severino apparently did not hesitate to promote his family's interests. To collect voluntary donations for the public schools, the assembly appointed a committee of two priests—Juan Felipe Ortiz (himself a member of the assembly) and Antonio José Martinez.[18] The task involved more than collecting cash. The next spring, Ortiz tallied up contributions amounting to forty-six pesos, four reales, and ninety-three sheep.[19] Padre Martínez may have succeeded in collecting contributions in Taos, too. He reportedly began operating a private school in Taos in November 1826,[20] and by 1831, if not before, Taos was one of six towns in New Mexico that employed a teacher to operate a public primary school.[21]

Requests for land or resolution of disputes over land constituted the most common item of local business for the assembly during don Severino's term and gave assemblymen a measure of power in the affairs of their communities. Martínez, for example, was able to block one petition for land at Taos, explaining that the grant would prove damaging to holders of adjacent lands.[22]

The territory's meager budget also concerned the assembly, which happily found a new source of revenue after Mexico won independence from Spain. The border with the United States, a barrier for trade under Spain, became a source of revenue under independent Mexico. Mexican trade policy and tariff laws offered New Mexican officials opportunities to collect customs duties from American merchants. The tariffs also gave American merchants a motive to smuggle goods or to bribe officials—problems that involved Severino Martínez in his capacities as assemblyman and alcalde of Taos, as we will see in chapter 6.

The parish priest

For Severino Martínez, then, the winds of change had brought more representative institutions to New Mexico and given him an opportunity to participate in politics at the territorial rather than the merely local level. His son, the priest, followed his father's lead. Padre Martínez applauded Mexican independence,

Daguerreotype of Padre Martínez.
From the collections of Shirley and Ward Alan Minge.

celebrating Spanish America's freedom from Spanish "tyranny . . . ignorance, error, and slavery" and applauding a fellow parish priest, Miguel Hidalgo. Hidalgo had launched Mexico's independence movement on September 16, 1810; in 1832, in commemoration of that day, Padre Martínez compared Hidalgo to Jesus Christ. As God sent Christ "to effect the spiritual salvation of all peoples," so God sent Hidalgo "to establish liberty." Like Christ, "Hidalgo preached the doctrine of his decisions, attacked the tyrants, gave us his example, [and] at the last died at their hands for the good of his country."[23]

A staunch nationalist who thought of himself as "*de patria mexicana*,"[24] Padre Martínez participated in the new political system with vigor. Even without his father's influence, he would have ranked among the territorial elite by dint of his education and ordination. When, for example, the *diputación* summoned a "junta general" in 1823 to deliberate New Mexico's relationship to a new government in Mexico City, the assembly invited the entire *ayuntamiento* of Santa Fe, two representatives from each of the other *ayuntamientos* in New Mexico, all priests, and other "distinguished *vecinos*." The dignitaries who assembled in Santa Fe totaled forty-two—an elite that included Padre Martínez, who had returned just two months before from Durango.25

But Padre Martínez was no ordinary priest. A man of enormous ambition as well as talent and energy, he enjoyed whatever advantages local pride might grant to a native of the territory. Nor did he live in ordinary times. Mexico's independence from Spain provided favorable circumstances for Padre Martínez to advance his clerical career in a province once dominated by Franciscans. With the departure of many Spanish-born priests for Spain, Mexico suffered a severe shortage of priests—especially in frontier areas. Franciscans, moreover, had come under pressure to secularize their missions. Under the new regime, state-supported missions would become locally supported parishes headed by secular clergy, or *curas*, such as Padre Martínez.

He seemed eager for a permanent position in his home parish, but he had to travel a circuitous route to get there. In the fall of 1823 Padre Martínez served as temporary pastor of the parish of Tomé, south of Albuquerque, remaining there until the following spring. In the spring of 1826, following the death of his twelve-year-old daughter the previous November, he took charge of the newly secularized church of Santo Tomás de Abiquiú, his parents' former parish where he himself had been baptized.

Never shy about self-promotion or involving himself in politics, Padre Martínez had urged the New Mexico Assembly to secularize the mission at Taos in 1824 and put him in charge of it.26 The assembly had agreed to press the case for secularization and had petitioned the bishop in Durango to secularize five missions, including Taos. Implementation, however, did not come until the arrival of a bishop's vicar in 1826. Then, in July 1826, Padre Martínez moved from Abiquiú to replace the last Franciscan as the first secular priest of the parish of San Gerónimo de Taos.27 That year, it would appear, he also moved the parish headquarters from the Indian pueblo to the chapel of Guadalupe in Don Fernando de Taos, an arrangement the bishop of Durango confirmed in 1833.28

About the same time that he made the chapel of Guadalupe the parish headquarters in 1826, Padre Martínez most likely made Don Fernando his home. His house still stands today on what has come to be called Padre Lane, two blocks southwest of the plaza near the original site of the chapel of Guadalupe.29 Padre Martínez's house, or one nearby, may have been built by Severino Martínez and inherited by the padre.30 From 1826 on, Padre Martínez and the parish headquarters came to be closely associated with Don Fernando de Taos. That the Indian pueblo had served as parish headquarters was soon forgotten. Writing in 1831 Antonio Barreiro noted that "the priest always lives there [in Don Fernando de Taos] because it is the focal point of all the settlements" in the Taos Valley.³¹ Meanwhile, Don Fernando de Taos had also become a focal point for a large number of foreigners from the United States—*extranjeros* who began to transform the Taos Valley.

Notes

1. Governor Melgares to the *alcaldes constitucionales*, Santa Fe, April 9, 1821. Ritch Papers, no. 73, Huntington Library, San Marino, California, cited in David J. Weber, *The Mexican Frontier, 1821–1846: The American Southwest under Mexico* (Albuquerque: University of New Mexico Press, 1982), 293, n. 9.

2. David J. Weber, ed. and trans., "An Unforgettable Day: Facundo Melgares on Independence," *NMHR* 48 (January 1973):29, 43, nn. 6 and 7. Severino did not identify himself as the alcalde, but he signed each document "*queda publicada y copiada en este de mi cargo*"—a notation that he would only have made had he been the alcalde, following the orders of the governor to publish the news in his district, in SANM, roll 20, frames 649 and 651. These appear to be the only documents in SANM that identify the alcalde of Taos in 1821.

3. Weber, *The Mexican Frontier*, 5.

4. For the curious evolution of the *diputación*, see Weber, *The Mexican Frontier*, 16–17, 19, 22, 27.

5. Lansing B. Bloom, "New Mexico Under Mexican Administration [part III]," *Old Santa Fe* 1 (January 1914):242, n. 147. Bloom gives the date as May in his text; March is correct. See MANM, roll 4, frames 841–42. The *diputación* existed in earlier forms in New Mexico, but this was the first under the new territorial system.

6. Minutes of the *diputación*, in MANM, roll 42, frames 277–78.

7. He missed the meeting of August 16, 1825. Sessions were held again in mid-September; in October the assembly did not meet. It met again in November, December, and January and March, April, May, and July, with don Severino in regular attendance.

8. If Taos followed prescribed procedures, then he would have been elected in December and taken office on January 1, 1825, for a one-year term. See the law of March 23, 1821, in Manuel Dublán and José María Lozano, eds., *Legislación mexicana . . .* (34 vols.; *Mexico: 1876–1904*), 1:543. See, too, Gilbert R. Cruz, *Let There Be Towns: Spanish Municipal Origins in the American Southwest, 1610–1810* (College Station: Texas A&M Press, 1988), 75–77.

9. Malcolm Ebright, "Manuel Martínez's Ditch Dispute: A Study in Mexican Period Custom and Justice," *NMHR* 54 (January 1979):31.

10. For Córdova, see Antonio José Martínez to Gov. Antonio Narbona, Taos, December 12, 1825, in MANM, roll 4, frames 764–67.

11. Minutes of the *diputación*, March 17, 1826, in MANM, roll 42, frames 385-86. For New Mexico's peculiar situation, see Weber, *The Mexican Frontier*, 26–28.

12. See David J. Weber, "El gobierno territorial de Nuevo México: La exposición del Padre Martínez 1831," *Historia Mexicana* 25 (October–December 1975):302–15. Antonio Barreiro, *Ojeada sobre Nuevo-Mejico* (1832), in H. Bailey Carroll and J. Villasana Haggard, eds. and trans., *Three New Mexico Chronicles . . .* (Albuquerque: The Quivira Society, 1942), 86.

13. Minutes of the *diputación*, November 16, 1825, in MANM, roll 42, frame 308.

14. Communication from Santiago Abreú read at the session of April 11, 1826, in MANM, roll 42, frame 391.

15. Minutes of the *diputación*, March 15, 1826, in MANM, roll 42, frames 378–88.

16. Wilson McGunnegle, letter from "San Francisco del Rancho (Taus) [*sic*], Province of New Mexico," June 30, 1823, St. Louis *Missouri Republican*, September 3, 1823; this reference is courtesy of Janet Lecompte.

17. George Sibley's diary, March 11, 1826, in Kate L. Gregg, ed., *The Road to Santa Fe: The Journal and Diaries of George Champlin Sibley* (Albuquerque: University of New Mexico Press, 1952), 156.

18. Minutes of the *diputación*, September 16, 1825, in MANM, roll 42, frame 301.

19. Minutes of the *diputación*, April 12, 1826, in MANM, roll 42, frames 394–95.

20. Angélico Chávez, *But Time and Chance: The Story of Padre Martínez of Taos, 1793–1867* (Santa Fe: Sunstone Press, 1981), 27.

21. Barreiro, *Ojeada*, 96.

22. Francisco Antonio Truxillo's request for land discussed at the session of March 18, 1826, in MANM, roll 42, frame 388.

23. Thomas J. Steele, S. J., "Padre Martínez Praises Padre Hidalgo," in Thomas J. Steele, *Folk & Church in Nineteenth Century New Mexico* (Colorado Springs: Hulbert Center for Southwestern Studies, 1993), 34, 39.

24. Antonio José Martínez, *Relación de Méritos del Presbítero Antonio José Martínez . . . cura engargado de Taos en el Departamento de Nuevo Mexico* (Taos: Impresa de su oficina á cargo de Jesus Maria Baca, 1838), 3.

25. Minutes of the *diputación*, in MANM, roll 42, frames 96-100. See, too, Lansing B. Bloom, "New Mexico Under Mexican Administration [part I]," *Old Santa Fe* 1 (October 1913):161–62.

26. Weber, *The Mexican Frontier*, 45–46, 59.

27. Chávez, *But Time and Chance*, 24–26, depending on Valdez, says that Martínez succeeded Fray José Mariano Sánchez Vergara; Connie Cortazar, "The Santa Visita of Agustín Fernández de San Vicente to New Mexico, 1826," *NMHR* 59 (January 1984):40, provides the context and explains that the vicar Fernández de San Vicente suspended Fray Buenas (Buenaventura) Muro and replaced him with Martínez. See, too, Santiago Valdez, "Biography of Padre Antonio José Martínez, cura-pastor of Parish of Taos, N.Mex., A.D. 1877, by Santiago Valdez," Rev. Juan Romero, Trans. (unpublished manuscript, 1993), 22.

28. Angélico Chávez, *Archives of the Archdiocese of Santa Fe, 1678–1900* (Washington, D.C.: Academy of Franciscan History, 1957), 156; and John L. Kessell, *Missions of New Mexico Since 1776* (Albuquerque: University of New Mexico Press, 1980), 109–110. Weber, *The Mexican Frontier*, 59.

29. *Ayer y Hoy—Taos, New Mexico: Our Lady of Guadalupe Parish* (Los Lunas, N.Mex.: Saint Clement's Church, 1976), 3. The present church is not on the site of the original church, whose exact location, Corina Santistevan tells me (letter of July 1994), remains unknown. It was probably in the area of today's Guadalupe Plaza.

30. Before he died in 1827, Severino Martínez noted in his will that he owned in Taos "one house started in which five rooms are finished." Ward Alan Minge, ed. and trans., "The Last Will and Testament of Don Severino Martínez," *New Mexico Quarterly* 33 (Spring 1963):38. The house known today as the Martínez house, according to Workers of the Writers' Program of the Works Progress Administration in the State of New Mexico, comps., *New Mexico: A Guide to the Colorful State* (New York: Hastings House, 1940), 222, "occupies the site of his [Padre Martínez's] school for boys and girls."

31. Barreiro, *Ojeada*, 86

CHAPTER
❖ SIX

ON SEVERINO AND THE NORTH AMERICANS

Whatever Severino Martínez thought of the new political arrangements, their economic consequences surely must have pleased him. When Mexico broke free from Spain it also abolished Spanish restrictions on trade with foreign countries. Suddenly and surprisingly, New Mexicans and North Americans could trade legally with one another.

Pleased to purchase manufactured goods of high quality for lower prices than they could obtain from central Mexico, New Mexicans welcomed traders from the United States and their wide assortment of merchandise. "Mostly they carried cloth and clothing, ranging from plain cotton handkerchiefs to imported silk shawls," in the words of one historian, "but their loads also included tools, kitchen utensils, and household goods from pins to pens and from wallpaper to window glass."[1]

Ironware held special interest. Although New Mexico had a number of skilled blacksmiths, iron itself was in very short supply. "They are almost entirely destitute of artizan's tools of every description," the Santa Fe trader Augustus Storrs observed in 1824, "and their implements of agriculture, such as carts, ploughs, harrows, yokes, spades, &c. are universally destitute of the least advantage of iron-work."[2] Storrs overstated the extent of the New Mexicans' shortage of iron, which was real enough, and don Severino may have begun to acquire more iron implements after the opening of the Santa Fe trade. When he died in 1827 he owned a metal grate, a metal shovel, an iron spindle, and a number of scythes, hoes, axes, and pieces of iron.[3]

For their part, *norteamericanos* saw opportunities for high returns in the form of silver, mules, and furs. Thus, driven by a mutually beneficial exchange, the Santa Fe trade got under way in the same year that Mexico achieved its independence. In short order, the Santa Fe Trail extended well beyond Santa Fe, developing into the main commercial link between northern Mexico and the western United States. It also brought new opportunities for commercially minded New Mexicans—some of whom entered the Santa Fe trade themselves.[4]

Taos and the Santa Fe Trail

Taos benefited from the opening of the Santa Fe trade in 1821, even though the Santa Fe Trail did not pass through Taos. The main branch of the Santa Fe Trail ran along the edge of the High Plains, skirting the eastern edge of the Sangre de Cristo Mountains of northern New Mexico. Nonetheless, Americans and their goods quickly found their way to the remote Taos Valley, nestled on the western side of the mountains. Some travelers unburdened by wagons went directly to Taos by taking a detour on the High Plains, turning westerly at the Cimarron River or at Ocaté Creek and crossing the Sangre de Cristos over the rugged Taos Pass. On the western slope of the mountains they followed the Río Fernando de Taos into Don Fernando de Taos itself (the same route by which Spanish officials a few years before feared that *norteamericanos* would invade the Taos Valley).[5] Most Americans remained on the main road all the way to Santa Fe but then scattered to different locales. Taos was their most popular destination in New Mexico.

During the years that New Mexico belonged to independent Mexico—1821 to 1846—more North Americans seem to have made their homes in Taos than in Santa Fe. Taos had several advantages for those foreigners. First, they felt at home amid its well-watered farms. Second, they believed they could live there less expensively than in the capital.[6] Third, they found Taos an attractive place for smuggling since it lacked a customshouse. Americans who trapped beaver had a special appreciation for the location of Taos. They found it convenient to both the southern Rockies, where they trapped, and to the Santa Fe Trail, the source of supplies and the chief conduit for sending out legally or illegally acquired beaver pelts. At the same time, Taos was distant from officials in Santa Fe, who tried to regulate foreign trappers after 1824.[7] In short, as one visitor from the United States noted in 1825, Don Fernando de Taos was "the nearest of the Mexican settlements, the most northern and the most abundant in provisions for man and beast."[8]

At "Touse" or "Taus," as some phonetically spelled it, a mountain man or merchant could pass the dead of winter or heat of summer in relative comfort, without having to journey back to Missouri. So many Americans made Taos home that in 1826, only five years after the opening of the Santa Fe trade, New Mexico's Gov. Antonio Narbona complained that the community's remote location "on the edge of our populated area" had made it a "refuge which many take advantage of without giving knowledge of their presence."[9] Taos, Antonio Barreiro observed in 1831, "is celebrated also for its commerce and because it is used as a common point of contact by large companies which come from the United States to hunt beaver; it is also used as a focal point by other traders."[10]

The Taos Valley, then, benefited economically from the new order. Within a decade after independence, the relatively young town of Don Fernando de Taos took its place alongside Santa Fe, Albuquerque, and Santa Cruz as one of New Mexico's four most important communities, eclipsing older towns such as Abiquiú.[11] The Martínez family had done well to move to Taos, where they prospered as the town grew in importance.

THE ALCALDE AND THE EXTRANJEROS

As alcalde of Taos, responsible for enforcing the laws that foreigners, or *extranjeros*, sought to circumvent, Severino Martínez came to understand the American influence in his community all too well. Soon after don Severino began his term as alcalde on January 1, 1825, he became involved in a controversy involving François Robidoux, one of several brothers from a Missouri clan who trapped and traded throughout the West in the 1820s and 1830s. In the autumn of 1824 Robidoux had arrived in Taos at the head of a small party of trappers and traders. There he soon ran into trouble with New Mexican authorities, who confiscated some of his goods because they suspected him of selling guns to hostile Indians.

On January 14, 1825, François Robidoux asked Alcalde Martínez to clear his name of this "slanderous accusation." Since he had taken up residence in Taos on November 25 of the previous year, Robidoux wrote, "there has not been committed, on the part of my people or myself, any disorder, scandal, or any controversy." To the contrary, he claimed, "harmony and fraternity" had characterized his relations with his neighbors in Taos. He and his associates had always respected the laws, the authorities, and the local customs and had, indeed, "adapted themselves" to them.[12] In fact, François would continue to adapt so well that the next year a local woman, Luisa Romero, would give birth to his daughter.[13]

Robidoux asked Martínez and the town council to certify his good behavior to the governor himself. He hoped that the governor would reveal the identity of the person who slandered him, bring that person to justice, and "clear our reputation . . . which every honorable man must carefully defend." Robidoux must have enjoyed considerable influence with Severino Martínez, who called a meeting of the seven-member *cabildo* on January 14, the very day that Robidoux wrote his letter. "In order to serve justice," Martínez and the other members of the town council certified the accuracy of Robidoux's claims.[14]

Six weeks later, Gov. Bartolomé Baca ordered Severino Martínez to return all of Robidoux's embargoed goods. Governor Baca's instructions to Alcalde Martínez on that occasion suggest the nature of the "slanderous accusation" against Robidoux. Foreigners who traded with "savage tribes," Baca wrote, should not enter Indian country with excessive arms, including "lances, powder, balls, flints, etc." Alcalde Martínez, Baca said, should permit the *extranjeros* to carry powder and ball sufficient only for their own defense.[15]

Since so many Americans entered and left New Mexico via Taos and since Taos lacked a customs officer, Martínez operated under special orders to keep tabs on them. In the spring of 1825 the territorial customs collector, Juan Bautista Vigil y Alarid, temporarily deputized Martínez and his associate, Rafael Luna, as border guards. Vigil ordered them to use militia to intercept American traders and examine their invoices, merchandise, passports, and other papers. Following this inspection, Martínez was to store the merchandise until Vigil appraised and taxed it. All appraisals, Vigil said, would ordinarily be conducted in Santa Fe, but he would travel to Taos if foreigners put their request in writing and paid his travel expenses in advance. When foreigners requested Vigil's services in Taos, Martínez was to collect the necessary passports, other papers, and the travel advance and forward them to Vigil in Santa Fe. Martínez should not permit the sale of foreign-made merchandise without a license, Vigil ordered, nor should he tolerate smuggling. Martínez should confiscate suspected contraband and begin judicial proceedings immediately.[16]

Vigil had good reason to urge Martínez to prevent foreigners from smuggling, for the practice seems to have been well established by 1825. That October, for example, Sylvestre Pratte hid some of his merchandise on the east side of the Sangre de Cristos before crossing over to Taos. Entering Taos with his remaining merchandise, he paid sufficient customs duties to give his enterprise the appearance of propriety. As the chronicler of his expedition noted, the alcalde, then Severino Martínez, "asked us for the invoice of our goods, which we showed him, and paid the customary duties on them."[17] Unbeknown to Martínez, Pratte planned to return for his cache at a later date and pass the contraband off as legal imports.

Martínez apparently took his responsibilities as a customs officer seriously. George Sibley, who arrived in Taos in late October 1825 as head of a U.S. survey party assigned to mark the Santa Fe Trail, noted in his diary that he left his lodgings on the day of his arrival to look for a house to rent on the outskirts of town:

> *On my Return found the Principal Alcalde & his Son the Curate [Antonio José] waiting for me. The[y] had waited on me officially to enquire my business, &c. which I very briefly explained to him & informed him that I intended Soon to inform the Governor that I had arr[ive]d & the object of my visit & they then departed.*[18]

Sibley had come to Taos directly, skirting Santa Fe and bringing wagons over the Sangre de Cristos—an event that if not the first, as he believed, was highly unusual.[19] Before Sibley had a chance to inform the governor of his business, it seems likely that don Severino had sent his own report.

The Robidoux-Vigil Imbroglio

Severino Martínez's encounters with foreigners did not always go so smoothly. The next month, in November 1825, François Robidoux showed up in Taos once again, having returned to Missouri over the summer. Traveling this time with three of his brothers, Antoine, Michel, and Louis, François brought his merchandise directly into Taos, avoiding the customshouse at Santa Fe.[20] This time, however, the territory's customs inspector, Juan Bautista Vigil y Alarid, traveled from Santa Fe to Taos to deal directly with Robidoux. When Vigil demanded his fee for the trouble of traveling to Taos to collect the customs duties, Robidoux balked. Vigil responded by confiscating seven bundles of his merchandise on the grounds that Robidoux had not listed them on his *factura*, or bill of lading. Robidoux protested. His brother, Michel, he said, had the goods listed on the proper papers and would arrive within two hours, but Vigil refused to wait.[21] Vigil impounded the merchandise, placed it for safekeeping in the house of Alcalde Severino Martínez, and returned to Santa Fe. Robidoux followed Vigil to the capital, hoping to persuade the governor to intercede on his behalf.[22]

During these contretemps at Taos, Severino Martínez had been in Santa Fe, fulfilling his duties as a member of the *diputación*. François Robidoux found Martínez there on November 17 and persuaded him to take his side in the dispute with Vigil. Visiting Vigil at his home, with Robidoux in tow, don Severino flexed his muscles. As alcalde of Taos, he told Vigil, he enjoyed power to order the return of Robidoux's merchandise "the same as if he were in Taos."[23] The next day, on November 18, Vigil ordered Rafael Luna of Taos to release Robidoux's property, explaining that Robidoux had produced the proper *factura*.[24] Perhaps he had or perhaps Vigil did not want to cross Severino Martínez.

Neither Vigil nor don Severino had heard the last of the matter. While Robidoux returned to Taos to retrieve his goods from Martínez's house, Martínez remained in Santa Fe, where the *diputación* continued to meet. Vigil's treatment of the Robidoux brothers at Taos had brought to a head long-simmering grievances against Vigil, and discussion of his ability to carry out his duties dominated the meetings of the *diputación* into January. Next to the governor, Vigil may have been the most powerful individual in the territory. He held an astonishing number of positions in the autumn of 1825: territorial treasurer, administrator of internal revenues and customs, tax collector, alcalde of Santa Fe, and secretary of the *diputación*.[25] Following the episode with Robidoux, the *diputación* quickly stripped Vigil of his post as secretary and then considered further action. Severino Martínez, who clearly reflected the views of his fellow assemblymen, argued that "experience has shown that don Juan Bautista Vigil is not capable of carrying out so many responsibilities," and he cited the delays that Americans had suffered at Taos while waiting for Vigil's arrival.[26]

An investigation into Vigil's conduct in the Robidoux affair soon suggested that Vigil had abused the power of his office and accepted payments under the table.[27] On December 19, Gov. Antonio Narbona sent the results of that investigation, together with other evidence of Vigil's mismanagement and peculation, to Chihuahua and asked for Vigil's suspension as territorial treasurer. Unwilling to wait while the wheels of bureaucracy turned, the *diputación* continued to consider the case through the holidays and into the new year. Reflecting the views of the majority of his colleagues, on January 3, 1826, Severino Martínez urged that Vigil be suspended from all offices while higher authorities reviewed the evidence.[28] The assembly took that step on January 11—its judgment eventually sustained by authorities in Mexico City.[29]

In 1826, with the coming of the new year, don Severino's duties as alcalde and assemblyman came to an end. For the year and a half of life that would remain for him, he could turn his attention back to his own affairs. Maintaining vigilance over the foreigners in Taos, though, did not end for the Martínez family.

In the spring of 1826, when Governor Narbona needed an agent in Taos to carry out an especially delicate task involving foreigners, he turned to the aging Severino's son, the priest. The governor asked Padre Martínez to locate and intercept any letters that Americans in Taos or their servants might be carrying to Manuel Escudero. Escudero, a Mexican attorney then in the United States, had come under suspicion for engaging in private diplomacy with the U.S. government. The success of this covert operation, Narbona told Padre Martínez, depended on his ability to carry it out quietly. He should keep his instructions a secret and not reveal them to anyone, not even to the alcalde of Taos himself.[30]

Mexicans and americans

Little record remains of how New Mexico's *vecino* regarded the Anglo-American newcomers in the 1820s, except that they greeted them warmly. "In all the principal towns the arrival of the Americans is a source of pleasure, and the evening is dedicated to dancing and festivity," noted Augustus Storrs, who traveled directly to Taos in the spring of 1824.[31] Similarly, James Ohio Pattie described a welcoming reception in Taos the next year: "Although appearing as poorly . . . they are not destitute of hospitality; for they brought us food, and invited us into their houses to eat, as we walked the streets."[32]

However hospitable their hosts, many of the Anglo Americans who arrived in Taos harbored views of racial and ethnic superiority toward Mexicans, whom they commonly regarded as indolent, corrupt, superstitious, and immoral. Imbued with the racial prejudices of his day, Pattie had described

Severino Martínez as "a man of swarthy complexion having the appearance of pride and haughtiness." As his party paid the required customs duties to don Severino, Pattie noted:

> *The door-way of the room, we were in, was crowded with men, women and children, who stared at us, as though they had never seen white men before. There being, in fact, much to my surprise and disappointment, not one white person among them.*[33]

To trapper Rufus Sage, who drew his conclusions from a brief visit to Taos in 1842, New Mexicans seemed a "mongrel race" and a "degenerate people": "Possessed of little moral restraint, and interested in nothing but the demands of present want, they abandon themselves to vice, and prey upon one another and those around them."[34]

At best, the *extranjeros* initially regarded New Mexico and the New Mexicans as exotic. Taos reminded Albert Pike of an "oriental town" when he saw it for the first time in 1831, "with its low, square, mud-roofed houses and its two square church towers, also of mud."[35] Pike felt transported "into a different world" and so, like other visitors, described the world of Severino Martínez and its inhabitants more vividly for his readers than he might have if New Mexico had seemed less strange:

> *Everything is new, strange, and quaint: the men with their pantalones of cloth, gaily ornamented with lace, split up on the outside of the leg to the knee, and covered at the bottom with a broad strip of morocco; the jacket of calico; the botas of stamped and embroidered leather; the zarape [serape] or blanket of striped red and white; the broad-brimmed hat, with a black silk handkerchief tied round it in a roll; or in the lower class, the simple attire of breeches of leather reaching only to the knees, a shirt and a zarape; the bonnetless women, with a silken scarf or a red shawl over their heads.*[36]

Customs as well as dress seemed strange to the Americans. Women drank, gambled, and smoked in public. Different classes seemed to mingle at a dance, or *fandango*, which Americans commonly attended. At Taos, Pike "saw the men and women dancing waltzes, and drinking whisky together; and in another room, I saw the montibank open. It is a strange sight—a Spanish fandango."37

For many visitors from the United States, however, the strange became the familiar. Overwhelmingly male, American visitors often found New Mexican women attractive. Some *americanos*, who took up permanent residence in New Mexico, married *vecinas*, especially in the Taos Valley. At Don Fernando de Taos, men such as Charles Bent, Charles Beaubien, Alexander Branch, Kit Carson, and Stephen Louis Lee lived with local women and raised their families; nearby, at Ranchos de Taos, John Rowland, William Workman, and other *extranjeros* lived with their New Mexican wives.38 Indeed, more than three-fourths of church-sanctioned marriages between Americans and Mexicans in New Mexico's Mexican era took place in the Taos Valley—that magnet for foreigners.39

Still, contempt did not always fade before familiarity. Charles Bent, a prominent merchant who made Taos his home and took a Mexican woman as his common-law wife, issued a scathing judgment of his neighbors after nearly two decades of living among them. "The Mexican character is made up of stupidity, obstinacy, ignorance, duplicity, and vanity," Bent wrote in a private letter in 1845.40 In another revealing letter, Bent sarcastically described Padre Martínez as "the greate Literry Marteanes . . . his greate name deserves to be written in letters of gold in all high places that this gaping and ignorant multitude might fall down and worship it."41

How the Martínez family responded to the *extranjeros* settling rapidly in their midst in the 1820s can only be imagined. The ethnocentrism and racism of some Anglo Americans could not have escaped the family's attention; don Severino must have experienced their scorn when he encountered Anglo Americans in his official capacity as alcalde in 1825.42 Conversely, many New Mexican oligarchs entered into advantageous alliances with Americans, and Severino's association with François Robidoux suggests that the two might have enjoyed a cordial or even mutually beneficial relationship.43 Certainly, Severino would have found it easier to deal with more culturally compatible French Americans like the Robidoux brothers than with Anglo Americans, but Severino Martínez did not live long enough to see the full impact that the *extranjeros* would make on Taos. We know much more about his son, Padre Martínez—an ardent Mexican nationalist who also admired the United States and who, in 1831, curiously bestowed the name "George" on the first of his illegitimate children.44

Notes

1. David J. Weber, *The Mexican Frontier, 1821–1846: The American Southwest under Mexico* (Albuquerque: University of New Mexico Press, 1982), 128.

2. Augustus Storrs and Alphonso Wetmore, *Santa Fé Trail, First Reports: 1825* (Houston: Stagecoach Press, 1960), 31. Marc Simmons and Frank Turley, *Southwestern Colonial Ironwork: The Spanish Blacksmithing Tradition from Texas to California* (Santa Fe: Museum of New Mexico Press, 1980).

3. Ward Alan Minge, ed. and Trans., "The Last Will and Testament of Don Severino Martínez," *New Mexico Quarterly* 33 (Spring 1963):47–52.

4. David A. Sandoval has explored this neglected subject. See his "Who Is Riding the Burro Now? A Bibliographical Critique of Scholarship on the New Mexican Trader," in *The Santa Fe Trail: New Perspectives. Essays in Colorado History* 6 (1987):75–92, and his "Gnats, Goods, and Greaser: Mexican Merchants on the Santa Fe Trail," in Marc L. Gardner, ed., *The Mexican Road: Trade, Travel, and Confrontation on the Santa Fe Trail* (Manhattan, Kans.: Sunflower University Press, 1989), 22–31.

5. Albert Pike, *Prose Sketches and Poems Written in the Western Country*, David J. Weber, ed. (Albuquerque: Calvin Horn, 1967), 19, 22–25; and Matthew C. Field, *Matt Field on the Santa Fe Trail*, John E. Sunder, ed. (Norman: University of Oklahoma Press, 1960), 166–75. See, too, Blanche C. Grant, *When Old Trails Were New: The Story of Taos* (New York: Press of the Pioneers, 1934), 45.

6. Angélico Chávez, "New Names in New Mexico, 1820–1850," *El Palacio* 64 (September–October 1957):292; on the cost of living, see George Sibley's diary, October 13, 1825, in Kate L. Gregg, ed., *The Road to Santa Fe: The Journal and Diaries of George Champlin Sibley* (Albuquerque: University of New Mexico Press, 1952), 113.

7. David J. Weber, *The Taos Trappers: The Fur Trade in the Far Southwest, 1540–1846* (Norman: University of Oklahoma Press, 1971), 93-94 and passim.

8. Field notes of Joseph C. Brown, U.S. Surveying Expedition, in Archer B. Hulbert, ed., *Southwest on the Turquoise Trail* (Denver: Steward Commission of Colorado College and the Denver Public Library, 1933), 129.

9. For the quote, and the strategic location of Taos for mountain men, see Weber, *Taos Trappers*, 8–9.

10. Antonio Barreiro, *Ojeada sobre Nuevo-Mejico* (1832), in H. Bailey Carroll and J. Villasana Haggard, eds. and trans., *Three New Mexico Chronicles . . .* (Albuquerque: The Quivira Society, 1942), 87.

11. Ibid., 84.

12. François Robidoux to Severino Martínez, San Fernando, January 14, 1825, Ritch Papers, no. 82, Huntington Library, San Marino, California. See Weber, *Taos Trappers*, 87. The date when Robidoux's goods were confiscated is not clear nor is the official who did it; perhaps it was Martínez's predecessor as the alcalde of Taos.

13. Born on January 30, 1826. See Weber, *Taos Trappers*, 88.

14. Severino Martínez, José Antonio Suaso (*secretario de cabildo*), Vicente Trujillo, Blas Trujillo, Juan Trujillo, Pablo Lucero, José Antonio Alarid, Juan del Carmen Romero, and Francisco Valdez, San Fernando, 14 January 1825, whose statement appears on the bottom of Robidoux to Martínez, San Fernando, January 14, 1825, Ritch Papers, no. 82, Huntington Library, San Marino, California.

15. Bartolomé Baca to the alcalde of Taos, March 3, 1825, in MANM, roll 4, frame 814. Baca referred to the Indians as "*naciones gentiles.*"

16. Juan Bautista Vigil, instructions to Rafael Luna and Severino Martínez, Santa Fe, April 20, 1825, in MANM, roll 4, frames 776–78. See, too, Weber, *Taos Trappers*, 93. Vigil termed Martínez and Luna "*Resguardos* and *contraresguardos.*" Foreigners were to pay duties called "*derechos de internación y de consumo.*"

17. Timothy Flint, ed., *The Personal Narrative of James O. Pattie of Kentucky*, intro. and notes by Milo Milton Quaife (Chicago: Lakeside Press, R. R. Donnelley & Sons, 1930), 54–55. Pattie's dates at this point are a year off—he reached Taos on October 26, 1825. Weber, *Taos Trappers*, 93, n. 37.

18. George Sibley's diary, October 30, 1825, in Gregg, *Road to Santa Fe*, 113.

19. Ibid., 111.

20. Weber, *Taos Trappers*, 88–89.

21. On this point, see the testimony of Rafael Luna, Taos, December 14, 1825, in the investigation of the conduct of Juan Bautista Vigil as *administrador de alcabalas*, in MANM, roll 4, frames 1061–62. My account is based on this and other testimony in the case. See, too, Weber, *Taos Trappers*, 93–94.

22. Testimony of François Robidoux, Taos, December 14, 1825, in the investigation of the conduct of Juan Bautista Vigil as *administrador de alcabalas*, in MANM, roll 4, frame 1056.

23. Testimony of Manuel Alvarez, Nuestra Señora de Guadalupe de la Joya in the *partido* de San Juan, December 13, 1825, ibid., frame 1053.

24. Copy of Vigil's note to Luna to release the goods, Santa Fe, November 18, 1825, ibid., frame 1064.

25. For a summary of these offices and an explanation of their duties, see Wayne A. Harper, "Juan Bautista Vigil y Alarid: A New Mexican Bureaucrat, 1792–1866" (M.A. thesis, Brigham Young University, 1985), 24–32. His first three titles, respectively: *comisario subalterno del territorio, administrador de rentas*, and *alcabalero*.

26. Minutes of the *diputación* session of November 21, 1825, in MANM, roll 42, frame 328.

27. Investigation of the conduct of Juan Bautista Vigil as *administrador de alcabalas*, in MANM, roll 4, frames 1049–71.

28. Minutes of the *diputación*, session of January 3, 1826, in MANM, roll 42, frame 360.

29. The best account of this is in Harper, "Juan Bautista Vigil," chapters 2 and 3.

30. Antonio Narbona to Presbítero Antonio Martínez, Santa Fe, April 10, 1826, Read Collection, no. 178, in SRCA. For Escudero, see especially William R. Manning, *Early Diplomatic Relations Between the United States and Mexico* (Baltimore: Johns Hopkins, 1916), 176–79. Unaware of the nature of the Escudero enterprise, E. A. Mares misunderstood this document: Mares, "Padre Martínez: New Perspectives from Taos," in *Padre Martínez: New Perspectives from Taos* (Taos: Millicent Rogers Museum, 1988), 24. Ray John de Aragon, *Padre Martinez and Bishop Lamy* (Las Vegas, N. Mex.: Pan-American Publishing, 1978), 10, blatantly distorted the meaning of the document, claiming that it says that Martínez would serve as "consulman for the Americanas . . . because of his knowledge of the English language." The document, whose location Aragon fails to cite, says no such thing. For other misreadings, see Juan Romero with Moises Sandoval, *Reluctant Dawn: Historia del Padre A. J. Martínez, Cura de Taos* (Los Angeles: Mexican American Cultural Center, 1976), 22; and Angélico Chávez, *But Time and Chance: The Story of Padre Martínez of Taos, 1793–1867* (Santa Fe: Sunstone Press, 1981), 28.

31. Storrs and Wetmore, *Santa Fé Trail, First Reports*, 19, 20.

32. Flint, *Personal Narrative of James O. Pattie*, 55.

33. Ibid., 54–55.

34. Quoted in David J. Weber, *Foreigners in Their Native Land: Historical Roots of the Mexican Americans* (Albuquerque: University of New Mexico Press, 1973), 73–75.

35. Albert Pike, *Prose Sketches and Poems Written in the Western Country (With Additional Stories)*, David J. Weber, ed. (1st ed., 1967; College Station: Texas A&M Press, 1987), 147.

36. Ibid., 148.

37. Ibid.

38. Rebecca McDowell Craver, *The Impact of Intimacy: Mexican-Anglo Intermarriage in New Mexico, 1821–1846* (El Paso: Texas Western Press, 1982), 10–12.

39. Ibid., 8. Of eighty-nine church-sanctioned marriages in Craver's sample, seventy-two took place in Taos—home, too, to many common-law marriages.

40. Quoted in David J. Weber, "'Scarce More than Apes': Historical Roots of Anglo-American Stereotypes of Mexicans," in David J. Weber, ed., *New Spain's Far Northern Frontier: Essays on Spain in the American West, 1540–1821* (Albuquerque: University of New Mexico Press, 1979), 296.

41. Charles Bent to Manuel Alvarez, Taos, January 30, 1841, [Frank D. Reeve, ed.], "The Charles

Bent Papers," *NMHR* 29 (October 1954):313–14. For the context, see David Lavender, *Bent's Fort* (Garden City, N.Y.: Doubleday, 1954), 249–51.

42. See, for example, the haughty way in which George Sibley treated Pedro Martínez, the "deputy alcalde" at Ranchos de Taos. Sibley to Martínez, August 19 and 23, 1826, in "Editorial Notes," *NMHR* 9 (January 1934):94–97. Weber, *Foreigners in Their Native Land*, 60–61.

43. On this question, see Manuel G. Gonzales, *The Hispanic Elite of the Southwest* (El Paso: Texas Western Press, 1989).

44. Chávez, *But Time and Chance*, 37, 73–74, 80–81.

CHAPTER
❖ SEVEN

THE ATRIARCH'S LEGACY

IN JUNE 1827, Severino Martínez suffered his last illness. Sick, but of sound mind, according to witnesses, he completed his last will and testament on June 8. He died later that month after his son, Antonio José, administered the sacraments of penance, extreme unction, and communion. Don Severino went to his reward having looked after his worldly affairs and having received all of the blessings that his faith could bestow upon him. From the grave he would also see that some of his worldly goods be used for his own spiritual well-being and for those less fortunate. He specified in his will that his estate pay for thirty low masses "for the benefit of my soul" and that twenty pesos of alms be given to the poor as a final act of charity.[1]

On June 29, 1827, don Severino was buried in the church of Our Lady of Guadalupe in the parish of San Gerónimo de Taos, as he ordered in his will. Although Antonio José served then as pastor of the parish, he did not officiate at his father's funeral. Instead, Father Juan Felipe Ortiz, whom Antonio José knew from his days at the seminary in Durango, came up from the parish of San Juan to preside over the service. Severino's body was interred in the nave of the church, of which he had been a benefactor—a "*bienhechor*," as his son noted in the burial register.[2]

Last will and testament

The day after the burial, on June 30, the two executors of don Severino's will met formally—his son-in-law, José Manuel Martínez, married to Severino's younger daughter Juana María and then serving a term as alcalde of Taos, and Severino's son, Antonio José.[3] The alcalde and the priest began to fulfill the terms of the will, authorizing expenditures for the burial and the masses to be said over the course of the next year. A few days later, on July 2, the two executors met again to begin to appraise and distribute the property—a process they did not complete until February 20, 1829.

Severino's tightly written four-page will, and the twenty-two pages that explain the terms of its settlement, constitutes an extraordinary source for historians. In the New Mexico of that era, as historian Ward Alan Minge has explained, the Severino Martínez will was "unusual both for its detail and for the careful accounting of its settlement. None of the few known wills of the time are accompanied with a comparable itemized listing with appraisals or such a thorough explanation of final property disposal."[4] The documents not only reveal much about the possessions of the Martínez family at the time of the patriarch's death but they also provide an unusual window onto the material world of other well-to-do *vecinos* of that time and place.

Spanish-Mexican custom and law entitled married women to retain their own private property within a marriage, and so don Severino had instructed that his wife's property be separated from his. Women, under Spanish-Mexican law, also owned half of the assets that the couple acquired during their marriage—their *gananciales*.[5] Thus, don Severino ordered that he and doña María's community property be divided into two parts, "one part recognized as assets [*por ganancial*] belonging to my wife, and the other . . . as my estate." His executors followed out those instructions. In distributing the sheep, for example, they first gave doña María "her half" before dividing up the rest.

Apart from specific bequests of land to two family servants, María Gertrudis and María Dolores, and payments designated for burial and religious purposes, don Severino divided his half of the assets among his six children. By then, all were married except for Antonio José, the widower-priest, and Juan Pascual, the youngest. Since Severino had not incurred any expenses for a marriage for Juan Pascual, the executors were to grant him a somewhat larger share of the estate—"it being the duty of the widow [María del Carmel] to see to his marriage with the help of this."6

Two years later, the children received their mother's estate when María del Carmel followed her husband to the grave. During the short illness that preceded her death, Padre Martínez had administered to her the sacraments of penance, extreme unction, and communion, as he had for his father. On April 25, 1829, her body, too, was buried in the nave of the church of Guadalupe. She merited that special place, her son wrote in the burial book, because "the sepulchre belonged to her ancestors, her deceased husband was in it, and she was the mother of the parish priest."7 María del Carmel died the very day that she was preparing her will in writing, but Padre Martínez noted that she made a verbal testament, bequeathing her property to her children.8 As her executor, Padre Martínez was still distributing her real estate at least as late as 1833.9

There was much, however, for the children to divide from don Severino's estate alone. His net worth came to 7,507 pesos, in personal possessions, real estate, herds, farm produce and equipment, and miscellaneous merchandise.10 His possessions included a saber with a silver scabbard, a large gilded mirror,11 and four plates, four spoons, four forks, and one silver cup.12 Cash on hand amounted to 800 pesos (much of it in official stamped silver); debtors owed the estate an additional 840 pesos.13 There were richer men in New Mexico, mainly in the Río Abajo, center of the great herds of sheep that constituted New Mexicans' major export commodity by the 1820s. Don Severino's sheep numbered more than a thousand at the time of his death, a substantial number but modest in comparison to the holdings of the richest men to the south.14 Nonetheless, don Severino certainly ranked among the most prosperous residents of New Mexico and perhaps the most prosperous in the Taos Valley.15

His real estate included structures as well as land. At the plaza of San Francisco del Ranchito he owned a mill and twenty-nine rooms in various houses, including his own. Two miles away, at Don Fernando de Taos, he had started building a house of which he had completed five rooms (his wife would receive that house, which might have then passed on to Padre Martínez after her death).16 At the plaza of Arroyo Hondo don Severino owned a room in the house of his niece, and at Santa Rosa and Rito Colorado near Abiquiú he owned still more rooms.

Don Severino apparently built this estate through diversified activities, including ranching, farming, and trading, as we have seen. Perhaps, too, he derived income by milling wheat for his neighbors. One American described the wheat grown in the Taos Valley as "of a superlative quality, and in such abundance, that, as is asserted, the crops have often yielded over a hundred fold."[17]

Sons of the patriarch

Don Severino's legacy also included his six children, two of them daughters about whom little is known.[18] The oldest, María Estefana, had married José Ignacio Lucero and apparently lived in San Miguel del Vado. Family tradition has it that the couple crossed the mountains by horseback every summer to visit Severino and María in Taos:

> *They would stay perhaps two weeks and Ignacio would get restless, wanting to return home. So Severino would give him a yearling colt, and Ignacio would leave through the mountains to San Miguel to take the foal back home, thus leaving Estefana to visit two or three more weeks with her family. And this was a custom that repeated itself several years.*[19]

María Estefana died at age thirty or thirty-one, within a year of her father's death; her five children received her share of the estate.[20]

The second daughter, Juana María, had married José Manuel Martínez in 1812 and apparently lived in the Taos Valley. Don Severino must have thought highly of her husband, whom he made coexecutor of his estate. José Manuel died in 1827 or 1828 while the will was being adjudicated;[21] several years later, Juana María married Juan Manuel Lucero, with Padre Martínez performing the ceremony.[22]

Don Severino also had four sons: Antonio José, José María de Jesús, José Santiago, and Juan Pascual Bailon—the last two known by their middle names, as Santiago and Pascual.

At least three of don Severino's sons—Antonio José, Santiago, and Pascual—followed his example and involved themselves in politics. The three brothers also farmed and raised sheep and other stock, as their father did before them, on lands they inherited from their father's estate. Even Padre Martínez, with his cleric's income and his well-known charity toward the poor, noted in 1838 that his own subsistence depended on income from "agriculture, common to the people of this department."[23] Indentured Indian servants must have continued to provide much of the labor for the Martínez brothers, as they did for many of the New Mexican *ricos* long after the United States acquired New Mexico and abolished slavery. According to family tradition, the servants included "Indian slaves, born on the hacienda, the descendants of Navajos who had been captured in early colonial campaigns."[24]

To the west of Taos, on land that might have belonged to Severino, the brothers tried to expand their farming operations by cutting a ditch from the Río Lucero to water a place described by one of their rivals, Charles Bent, as "land on the high prairie on the west side of this town about two miles direcly [sic] west of Pedro Martins residence." Padre Martínez and his family, Bent said in the spring of 1846, were trying to open this land, taking water from a source the Pueblos claimed.[25]

North of town, beyond Arroyo Hondo, the brothers also maintained interests in the family lands at San Cristóbal, but Indians made it difficult to work them. As Charles Bent explained in 1845, Padre Martínez "and his brothers have a greadeal [sic] of good land at this place which they are afraid to plant." The Martínez brothers hoped to solve the problem by persuading the government to establish a military post on the Río Colorado, the next river to the north of the San Cristóbal, but nothing came of their initiative.[26] After the United States acquired New Mexico in 1846 Antonio José, Santiago, and Pascual retained their interest in the San Cristóbal lands, where they tried to secure title.[27]

The brothers also expanded their father's ranching operations in new directions, using open range, to which they may or may not have held title, as was the custom. On the east side of the Sangre de Cristos, at a place called the Cerro de la Gallina, they ran cattle and sheep in large numbers. From that place, Utes ran off eight thousand sheep and four hundred head of cattle in early 1846, much if not all belonging to the three Martínez brothers. Charles Bent learned that Padre Martínez, who had been "lawding the Mexican Government and people to the skyes," had changed his tune after losing his livestock and "sayes the Government is fit for nothing, and hopes thare may soon be a chainge."[28] Pascual Martínez led a search party that returned empty-handed, but not until, as Bent put it, the group had a "hard fight, with Capt Whisky at Turlys [Turley's mill and distillery]. . . . Capt W gained the batl [battle], but not the field, as the most of them slept on it that night."[29]

Charles Bent, the author of these unflattering anecdotes about Padre Martínez and his brother Pascual, loathed the Martínez brothers and followed their activities closely. It is clear from Bent's comments that by the 1840s, if not before, three sons of don Severino—Antonio José, Santiago, and Pascual—had become the leading dynasty in Taos and exercised influence in Santa Fe as well; the patriarch's second son, José María de Jesús, has eluded the historical record.[30]

In Taos, Santiago Martínez played a role in town politics at least as early as 1828 and held the office of subprefect in 1837—the highest local office under a new constitution adopted the year before.[31] On the provincial level he served in the assembly at least once, in 1844, when he presided over that body.[32] Perhaps business interested him more than politics. In 1839 the secretary of the treasury in Mexico City appointed don Santiago as the agent of the Mexican National Bank in New Mexico, a position of sufficient importance that notification of his appointment went to officials throughout the territory.[33] Beyond that, little is known about Santiago Martínez.

More is known about Pascual, who eventually came to own the Martínez hacienda and who distinguished himself as the highest ranking officer in the Taos Valley in the years before the U.S. invasion of 1846.[34] In 1839, Gen. Antonio López de Santa Anna appointed Pascual a militia captain—a newly created office.[35] Pascual also served as a justice of the peace in 1845 and 1846, a position that enabled him to wield considerable local influence.[36]

As militia captain, Pascual Martínez made his influence felt beyond the Taos Valley even though his volunteer forces were still expected to equip themselves at their own expense and fight on their own time. In January of 1841, for example, Capt. Pascual Martínez received orders to proceed to Santo Domingo Pueblo with twenty-five of his best men, armed and supplied for eight days, in order to serve as part of a larger force that would celebrate a recent peace with Navajos.[37] At the same time, Martínez had been among those officers who received early intelligence of Texas plans to invade New Mexico in 1841 and annex it to the Lone Star Republic.[38] Pascual received a "cross of honor" from Santa Anna for his role in repelling the Texas invasion of New Mexico in 1841.[39]

More is known about Antonio José than any of the other brothers. By dint of temperament, training, intelligence, and his position as parish priest, the oldest brother became the leader of the triumvirate that ran Taos.[40] Padre Martínez, it would appear, tried to keep at least one of his brothers in a key office in Taos at all times while he manipulated local affairs from behind the scenes.[41] Until the U.S. takeover in the Mexican-American War, his manipulation succeeded. On the eve of the war, Charles Bent, who belonged to a rival faction in Taos, pronounced the Martínez family "in authority" in Taos.[42]

Bent and Padre Martínez were not only personal enemies but they represented different factions in local politics. Alarmed at growing foreign influence in the territory, Padre Martínez tried to block Americans like Bent from acquiring huge tracts of New Mexico real estate.⁴³ Bent thought Martínez a tyrant, a braggart, and a malicious busybody who "will spair no meanes to injure me."⁴⁴ Padre Martínez apparently believed that Bent, similarly, would spare no means to ruin him. To his delight, Bent recounted on one occasion how the padre's exaggerated fears led him to imagine that Bent had dug a tunnel from Bent's house "to the Church in which I had deposited three Kegs Powder, for the purpus of blowing them up on Good [F]riday."⁴⁵

The influence of the Martínez clan extended well beyond Taos in the era when New Mexico still belonged to independent Mexico. Padre Martínez himself founded primary and preparatory schools at Taos that launched the careers of a new generation of native-born clergy, and from 1835 to 1847 he operated the province's only printing press—one that he loaned on occasion to the central government. Like his father and his younger brother, Santiago, Antonio José served in the New Mexico Assembly but with greater frequency—in 1831–32, 1837–38, and 1845–46.⁴⁶

Padre Martínez also made his voice heard on the national scene. One of his missives to the central government in Mexico City concerned Americans such as Charles Bent, a resident of Taos and the proprietor of Bent's Fort, a trading post on the Arkansas River. In 1843, Martínez explained to President Antonio López de Santa Anna that Indian attacks upon settlements throughout northern Mexico had increased because Anglo Americans had constructed trading posts at points on the Arkansas and Platte rivers. By dealing in furs and hides, the American traders encouraged Indians to wasteful slaughter of game animals, especially buffalo. As their game declined, Martínez said, Apaches, Utes, Navajos, and Comanches increasingly stole livestock and crops from Mexican settlements, some Indians robbing stock from Mexicans in order to sell it to Americans. His humane solution: "civilize" the "barbaric" Indians, teaching them to become self-sufficient on their own farms and ranches.⁴⁷

The Martínez Brothers and the American Takeover

In September 1845, with tensions building between the United States and Mexico over the Americans' annexation of Texas that March, Capt. Pascual Martínez received orders to prepare the militia for an anticipated invasion by U.S. forces.⁴⁸ The next spring, in April 1846, as part of those preparations and in recognition of his "merits and distinguished service," Gov. Manuel Armijo ordered Pascual Martínez promoted from captain of militia forces (*auxiliaries*) to *coronel inspector*.⁴⁹ By late June, Colonel Martínez had organized three companies of militia, each with its respective captains and other officers. Like all soldiers in New Mexico, they suffered a severe shortage of arms and ammunition. The largest company consisted of ninety men, seventy of them with firearms. Company Two had seventy men, of whom forty possessed firearms. Company Three had fifty men, thirty of them with guns.⁵⁰

Meanwhile, the war that Governor Armijo had feared came to pass, although many weeks went by before he learned of it. On May 11, 1846, the United States declared war on Mexico. A month later, in mid-June, U.S. forces under Gen. Stephen Watts Kearny set out from Missouri for New Mexico. By the end of June rumors of his approach reached New Mexico. In early July, Governor Armijo ordered Colonel Martínez to cross over the Sangre de Cristos and check out a report that American forces were camped where the Santa Fe Trail crossed the Vermejo River.⁵¹ The report proved premature. Not until July 11 did Governor Armijo receive reliable intelligence of the impending American invasion. That day Armijo wrote to Colonel Martínez, "It is now positively known" that forces from the United States were advancing over the Santa Fe Trail to seize New Mexico. Governor Armijo ordered New Mexico's "most influential citizens" to come to Santa Fe to work on preparations for defense. Within three days of receipt of Governor Armijo's order, Colonel Martínez was to present himself before the governor in Santa Fe, bringing with him nine "prominent men" from Taos. The list of nine notables included three priests, Padre Martínez among them.⁵²

Careful preparations notwithstanding, Governor Armijo's pragmatism overcame his nationalism. Outgunned, he recognized a hopeless cause and opted to abandon New Mexico.⁵³ In mid-August American forces entered New Mexico without resistance and took possession of the province. Like many other members of the New Mexico oligarchy, Antonio José, Santiago, and Pascual Martínez may have felt chagrined and embarrassed over Governor Armijo's retreat.⁵⁴

The ease of the American conquest, however, proved illusory. By December New Mexicans had hatched a plot to regain their freedom—a patriotic action known as the Taos Rebellion of 1847. Some historians have supposed that Padre Martínez's influence was so great that he must have been among the leaders of the bloody resistance (just as some scholars presumed he had been a guiding force behind the violent Chimayó Rebellion of 1837).⁵⁵ Indeed, some prominent New Mexicans later accused all three Martínez brothers of meeting with other conspirators in December 1846 to plot the overthrow of the newly installed American government presided over by Charles Bent, and some accused Pascual of participating openly in the Taos revolt the next month.⁵⁶

These charges may have some validity, but they derive from hearsay, some of it recalled long after the event. The documentary record indicates only that Santiago Martínez served on the grand jury in April 1847 that indicted participants in the Taos Rebellion[57] and that Padre Martínez offered his house as a refuge for fugitives from the rebels and that he deplored the harshness of the punishments meted out to them after the rebellion failed.[58]

Following the United States acquisition of New Mexico, Pascual and Antonio José remained vulnerable to charges of disloyalty. In 1857, for example, a rumor spread that the brothers planned to lead an insurrection of native New Mexicans at Taos. Alerted to the danger by Kit Carson, the commander of nearby Cantonment Burgwin rode into Taos on the night of May 27 with a small contingent of troops. Arriving at the house of Padre Martínez, where the ringleaders supposedly had gathered, the American soldiers found the priest asleep.

At least fifteen similar false alarms sounded in Taos in the decade after the Treaty of Guadalupe Hidalgo (not all of them involving the Martínez brothers). Taos merchants apparently started some of these rumors in the hope of keeping troops stationed close to town where they could spend their salaries on local merchandise rather than pursuing Indians on distant frontiers of the territory. Then, too, some Anglo-American politicians found it in their interest to brand Mexican Americans as disloyal and therefore unfit for self-government.[59]

Whatever lingering suspicions about their loyalty, Pascual and Antonio José Martínez played roles as prominent under the new American government as they had under Mexico. In the immediate aftermath of the U.S. conquest of New Mexico, between 1846 and 1848, Padre Martínez vigorously promoted the transition to U.S. rule. Perhaps the most influential New Mexican of his day, in 1848 he was elected president of a convention called to petition the U.S. Congress to make New Mexico a territory; in 1849 a similar convention, called to draft a new government, elected him as president. When New Mexico became a territory in 1850, Padre Martínez served as president of the council, or upper house, of the first territorial assembly in 1851; in 1852 and 1855 he represented Taos as a member of the assembly but was not an officer. Even after he retired from the territorial legislature, Padre Martínez's adopted son, Santiago Valdez, and his brother, Pascual, represented Taos in the assembly and perhaps the family's interests as well.[60]

Padre Martínez is best remembered, however, for a quarrel with the French-born bishop of Santa Fe, Jean Baptiste Lamy, that culminated in 1857. Willa Cather's reimagining of that quarrel in her novel *Death Comes for the Archbishop* (1926) helped keep the memory of Padre Martínez alive among twentieth-century readers but also distorted his memory by vilifying him. The fictional Padre Martínez eclipsed the historical Padre Martínez and his extraordinary achievements. Even scholarly writers must reckon with Cather's imagination as they attempt to understand the padre's life.[61]

Fiction aside, the fact is that don Severino's most visible son had become an oversized figure for his time and place and a contradictory one: a village priest of great intellectual gifts and ego; a moralist with illegitimate children; a populist whose broad humanitarian vision and efforts to achieve political and ecclesiastical reform were often offset by arrogance and intolerance; and an ardent Mexican nationalist who led the way toward making New Mexico part of the United States.[62] Whatever his weaknesses, his strengths had made him the most important cultural force in New Mexico in the two decades prior to the Mexican War, as well as the province's most notable religious leader and a key political figure in both the Mexican and American eras. He was surely, as a historian has written, "one of the most remarkable men ever identified with the history of New Mexico."[63] As his life has been reconstructed in hagiography and biography, as well as in historical fiction, Padre Martínez has also become, in the words of historian Thomas Steele, "a numinous and fascinating figure, great man and great myth in one."[64]

At the same time that the bombastic priest of Taos gained influence and notoriety after the U.S. acquisition of New Mexico, his brother, Pascual, also wielded political power. Pascual represented Taos in a legislative assembly organized under the U.S. military government in 1847, the lower house of the first three territorial assemblies from 1851 to 1853, and the territorial council in 1855 and 1856.[65] In Taos itself, he involved himself as a political leader until at least the end of the Civil War, leadership that included providing cash and whiskey for compliant voters on election day.[66]

Pascual also continued his career as a militia officer in Taos. He served as an American officer in the early 1850s, just as he had once served Mexico.[67] As a rancher, he found it in his interest to continue to fight Indians, for Indian raids on livestock remained a problem in the Taos Valley long after the American occupation. In 1855, for example, while Pascual was away in Santa Fe, serving in the legislature, his brother Antonio José wrote to him from Taos: "With respect to the news of Apaches and other Indians, I believe that our animals are well protected in the most concealed areas with good pasture."[68] Pascual, according to family tradition, had a particular passion for horses and a herd that reportedly numbered in the thousands; he supplied some to the Union Army during the Civil War.[69]

Even as he ranched and served as a militia officer and legislator, Pascual carried on his father's mercantile trading business south to Chihuahua, family tradition suggests. He apparently also extended that tradition by trading eastward to St. Louis.⁷⁰

Until his death in 1882, Pascual made his father's house the headquarters for his manifold activities. Sometime during these years don Severino's great house had fallen entirely into Pascual's possession, perhaps as his older brothers died and he inherited their shares of their parents' legacy.

Notes

1. Ward Alan Minge, ed. and trans., "The Last Will and Testament of Don Severino Martínez," *New Mexico Quarterly* 33 (Spring 1963):36, 40. I have also consulted the original manuscript of the will.

2. Burial Book 39, Taos, 1827–50, pp. 10r–10v, in AASF, roll 42, frames 20–21, a copy kindly made for me by Professor Thomas Steele. Angélico Chávez, *But Time and Chance: The Story of Padre Martínez of Taos, 1793–1867* (Santa Fe: Sunstone Press, 1981), 29, summarized this document and called it to my attention.

3. The will identifies the marriage relationship and the fact that José Manuel (who signed his name Manuel) then served as alcalde. See, too, Chávez, *But Time and Chance*, 18.

4. Minge, "Last Will and Testament," 35.

5. Joseph W. McKnight, "Spanish Law for the Protection of Surviving Spouses in North America," *Anuario de historia del derecho español* 57 (1989):367–406, explains Spanish *gananciales* principles and their impact on American matrimonial property law. Janet Lecompte, "The Independent Women of Hispanic New Mexico, 1821–1846," *Western Historical Quarterly* 12 (January 1981):27.

6. Minge, "Last Will and Testament," 46.

7. "*En este curato de San Geronimo de Taos a los veinte y cinco dias del mes de Abril de 1829, yo el Presbitero don Antonio Jose Martinez, cura parroco del mismo, en el cuerpo de la iglesia de Nuestra Señora de Guadalupe, di sepultura ecclesiastica al cadaver de doña Maria del Carmel Santiestevan, esposa que fue del finado don Severino Martinez. Le administré los santos sacramentos de penitencia, extrema uncion y santo viatico por auxilio en su ultima enfermedad. Hiso verbal su testamento en favor de sus hijos y mandar de sus bienes que tenia, no por escrito porque la circunstancia no dio tregua; pues al tiempo en que se estaba fabricando, abrabiose su enfermedad, y murió en el mismo dia, y fué sepultada en el cuerpo de la iglesia, a merito de ser el sepulcro de sus mayores, y su difunto esposo en ella, y madre del cura mismo que soy el parroco, y para que conste lo firmé.*" Antonio José Martínez. This is not a literal transcription; I have modernized some of the punctuation and spelling; Burial Book 39, Taos, 1827–50, p. 45, in AASF, roll 42, frame 95, a copy kindly made for me by Professor Thomas Steele. Chávez, *But Time and Chance*, 30, summarizes this and called it to my attention.

8. Ibid.

9. In an inventory of land and houses that Juan Pascual Martínez inherited from both parents, Taos, March 8, 1833, Padre Martínez identified himself as the executor of the wills of both of his parents. Recorded May 7, 1909, in the Record of Wills and Testaments, Taos County, Book 8, pp. 427–28, office of the Taos County Clerk.

10. Minge, "Last Will and Testament," 56.

11. Ibid., 44, 54.

12. Ibid., 39.

13. Ibid.

14. The number of 1,552 given in Minge, "Last Will and Testament," 46, is an error. See above, chapter 2, n. 44. For the size of some other herds at this time, see Ward Alan Minge, "Efectos del País: A History of Weaving along the Río Grande," in *Spanish Textile Tradition of New Mexico and*

Colorado (Santa Fe: Museum of New Mexico Press, 1979), 23.

15. See, for example, the assets of Manuel Delgado, who died in 1815, summarized in John O. Baxter, *Las Carneradas: Sheep Trade in New Mexico, 1700–1860* (Albuquerque: University of New Mexico Press, 1987), 75; and Daniel Tyler, "The Personal Property of Manuel Armijo, 1829," *El Palacio* 80 (Fall 1974):45–48.

16. Minge, "Last Will and Testament," 38, 50.

17. Josiah Gregg, *Commerce of the Prairies*, Max L. Moorhead, ed. (1st ed., 1844; Norman: University of Oklahoma Press, 1954), 104.

18. The most basic information about Severino's descendants has yet to be recovered. The vagueness of genealogical work is suggested in Fred G. Martínez, *The Story of Antonio Severino Martínez y Lucero de Godoy and María del Carmel Santistevan* (Taos: Kit Carson Memorial Foundation Publications in History, no. 6, 1977), 3–4, 12–13.

19. Ibid., 6.

20. Minge, "Last Will and Testament," 51.

21. Ibid., 47.

22. At Taos on March 6, 1832. John O. Baxter, *Spanish Irrigation in Taos Valley* (Santa Fe: New Mexico State Engineer Office, 1990), 63.

23. Antonio José Martínez, *Relación de Méritos del Presbítero Antonio José Martínez . . . cura engargado de Taos en el Departamento de Nuevo Mexico* (Taos: Impresa de su oficina á cargo de Jesus Maria Baca, 1838), 30.

24. Ruth G. Fish, "La Hacienda de Don Pascual Is Located on Río de Pueblo Near Taos," *The Taos Review* (June 1, 1940). Fish based this statement on an interview with the widow of Severino's grandson, Agapito Martínez, doña Virginia Gonzáles de Martínez, "the last of the Martínez line to live in the house," who described her own servants. See, too, L. R. Bailey, *Indian Slave Trade in the Southwest* (Los Angeles: Westernlore Press, 1966).

25. Charles Bent to Manuel Alvarez, Taos, April 14, 1846, [Frank D. Reeve, ed.], "The Charles Bent Papers," *NMHR* 31 (April 1956):158.

26. Charles Bent to Manuel Alvarez, Taos, March 30, 1845, [Frank D. Reeve, ed.], "The Charles Bent Papers," *NMHR* 30 (October 1955):340–41.

27. See the inventory of land at San Cristóbal, which the executor had neglected to include in the inventory of 1833. Antonio José Martínez, Taos, December 14, 1849, recorded May 7, 1909, in the Record of Wills and Testaments, Taos County, Book 8, pp. 427–28, office of the Taos County Clerk.

28. Charles Bent to Manuel Alvarez, Taos, February 16, 1846, [Frank D. Reeve, ed.], "The Charles Bent Papers," *NMHR* 30 (October 1955):344. Editor Reeve identifies the Cerro de la Gallina as the Turkey Mountains, east of Fort Union. It may also have been closer to Taos, at Mount Gallinas, three miles northwest of Ocaté. In either case, I think it was a location to the east because the search party rode eastward from Taos, out along the Río Fernando de Taos.

29. Charles Bent to Manuel Alvarez, Taos, February 26, 1846, [Frank D. Reeve, ed.], "The Charles Bent Papers," *NMHR* 30 (October 1955):344.

30. The name of José María de Jesús appears on an 1835 list of Taos oligarchs, in Henry R. Wagner, "New Mexico Spanish Press," *NMHR* 12 (January 1937):17–18; John O. Baxter believes that a Jesús María Martínez who was elected Taos County's first probate judge in 1851 was Severino's son (Baxter to Weber, Santa Fe, August 29, 1994).

31. Certification of the election of "*electores*," Taos, August 17, 1828, Sender Collection, in SRCA, doc. 91, roll 1, frames 588–600, in which Santiago received the largest number of votes. Since the records of the town council are gone, we cannot fully reconstruct his civic career in Taos. Janet Lecompte, *Rebellion in Río Arriba, 1837* (Albuquerque: University of New Mexico Press, 1985), 47; and Lansing B. Bloom, "New Mexico Under Mexican Administration," *Old Santa Fe* 2 (July 1914):9.

32. Lansing B. Bloom, "New Mexico Under Mexican Administration," *Old Santa Fe* 2 (October 1914):159; and Minge, "Last Will and Testament," 33.

33. Prefect Juan Andrés de Archuleta, Río Arriba, to the *jueses de paz de* San Ildefonso, Cañada, San Juan, and Chama, February 24, 1840. Sender Collection, in SRCA, doc. 238a, roll 21, frames 335–36. See, too, ibid., frames 33–54.

34. Charles Bent to Manuel Alvarez, Taos, February 26, 1846, [Frank D. Reeve, ed.], "The Charles Bent Papers," *NMHR* 30 (October 1955):346.

35. The letter of appointment appears in translation in [George P. Anderson], *History of New Mexico: Its Resources and People*, 2 vols. (Los Angeles: Pacific States Publishing, 1907), 2:712. See, too, Bloom, "New Mexico Under Mexican Administration" (October 1914):134.

36. Charles Bent to Manuel Alvarez, Taos, March 30, 1845, and Bent to Alvarez, Taos, two letters of May 3, 1846, [Frank D. Reeve, ed.], "The Charles Bent Papers," *NMHR* 30 (October 1955):341, and *NMHR* 31 (April 1956):160–62. Pascual was also judge of the Second District of Arroyo Hondo in 1835 (Malcolm Ebright, "History of the Arroyo Hondo Grant," 6, citing as testimony in *Montoya v. Anderson*, Taos County civil case no. 79–106).

37. Antonio María Trujillo, *ayudante de armas* of the First District, Río Arriba, January 27, 1841, to *Capitán rural* Pascual Martínez, in PMP, no. 1.

38. Among family papers from Pascual was a letter from Manuel Armijo, Santa Fe, July 10, 1840, to Lt. Col. Juan Andrés Archuleta, with news of the Texas preparations, in PMP, no. 5.

39. Mexico, December 21, 1841, translation of the award in [Anderson], *History of New Mexico*, 2:712.

40. Charles Bent clearly saw Padre Martínez as the leader of the three. "He directs his brother the justice," Bent wrote to Manuel Alvarez, Taos, April 8, 1846, [Frank D. Reeve, ed.], "The Charles Bent Papers," *NMHR* 31 (April 1956):158.

41. Charles Bent to Manuel Alvarez, Taos, February 28, 1846, [Frank D. Reeve, ed.], "The Charles Bent Papers," *NMHR* 30 (October 1955):347.

42. Charles Bent to Manuel Alvarez, Taos, May 3, 1846, [Frank D. Reeve, ed.], "The Charles Bent Papers," *NMHR* 31 (April 1956):162.

43. David J. Weber, *The Mexican Frontier, 1821–1846: The American Southwest under Mexico* (Albuquerque: University of New Mexico Press, 1982), 193.

44. Charles Bent to Manuel Alvarez, Taos, April 14, 1846, [Frank D. Reeve, ed.], "The Charles Bent Papers," *NMHR* 31 (April 1956):157.

45. Ibid., 158–59. The source of the story, according to Bent, was Padre Martínez's sister.

46. Chávez, *But Time and Chance*, 35, 78. Ward Alan Minge, "Frontier Problems in New Mexico Preceding the Mexican War, 1840–1846" (Ph.D. diss., University of New Mexico, 1965), 325.

47. See the *Esposición que el presbítero Antonio José Martínez, cura de Taos de Nuevo México, dirije al Govierno del . . . Santa Anna . . .* (Taos: J. M. B., 1843), a rare ten-page imprint, is reproduced in facsimile in David J. Weber, ed., *Northern Mexico on the Eve of the United States Invasion: Rare Imprints . . .* (New York: Arno, 1976). For an earlier communication from Martínez to the central government, see David J. Weber, "El gobierno territorial de Nuevo México: La exposición del Padre Martínez 1831," *Historia Mexicana* 25 (October–December 1975):302–315, a work unnoted by students of the padre's life.

48. Diego Lucero to the "*capitanías*" of Don Fernando and Ranchos de Taos, *Prefectura del distrito del norte*, September 2, 1845, in PMP, no. 3.

49. Order of Gen. Manuel Armijo, governor and comandante general of the Department of New Mexico, Palacio de Gobierno, Santa Fe, April 22, 1846. The order was carried out on May 2, 1846, by Antonio María Trujillo, in PMP, no. 6.

50. Report of Pascual Martínez to Governor Armijo, June 27, 1846, in PMP, no. 7. On the general shortage of arms, see David J. Weber, ed. and trans., *Arms, Indians, and the Mismanagement of New Mexico: Donaciano Vigil, 1846* (El Paso: Texas Western Press, 1986), xii, 6–8.

51. José Pablo Gallegos to Col. P. Martínez, Taos, June 30, 1846, and Governor Armijo to Col. P. Martínez, Santa Fe, July 6, 1846. The document says "*puesto*" or "*punto*" de "*Bermejo*," in PMP, nos. 9 and 10.

52. Governor Armijo to Pascual Martínez, Santa Fe, July 11, 1846, and Armijo, "List of the Prominent Men who should come to this capital with Coronel Pascual Martínez," Santa Fe, July 11, 1846, in PMP, nos. 4 and 8. For July 11 as the day that Armijo received reliable information, see Minge, "Frontier Problems," 328–29.

53. Daniel Tyler, "Governor Armijo's Moment of Truth," *Journal of the West* 1 (April 1972):307–16.

54. See David J. Weber, *Foreigners in Their Native Land: Historical Roots of the Mexican Americans*

(Albuquerque: University of New Mexico Press, 1973), 121–25.

55. These general observations about Padre Martínez, and those that follow, are derived largely from Chávez, *But Time and Chance* (the best biography to date), and E. A. Mares, "The Many Faces of Padre Antonio José Martínez: A Historiographic Essay," in *Padre Martínez: New Perspectives from Taos* (Taos: Millicent Rogers Museum, 1988), 18–47.

56. Ralph Emerson Twitchell, *Old Santa Fe: The Story of New Mexico's Ancient Capital* (Santa Fe: New Mexican Publishing, 1925), 276; and Ralph Emerson Twitchell, *The History of the Military Occupation of the Territory of New Mexico . . .* (Denver: Smith-Brooks, 1909), 133. Twitchell, an attorney, made these charges based on hearsay evidence and they have been repeated, as by Paul A. F. Walter, "The First Civil Governor of New Mexico under the Stars and Stripes," *NMHR* 7 (April 1933):104.

57. Francis T. Cheetham, "The First Term of the American Court in Taos, New Mexico," *NMHR* 1 (January 1926):28.

58. Mares, "The Many Faces of Padre Antonio José Martínez," 27–30; and Arthur J. O. Anderson, "Taos Uprising Legends," *El Palacio* 8 (December 1946), 335, who presents varying interpretations of Padre Martínez's role.

59. Thomas J. Steele, S.J., "Kit Carson and Padre Martínez," in Thomas J. Steele, S.J., *Folk & Church in Nineteenth Century New Mexico* (Colorado Springs: Hulbert Center for Southwestern Studies, 1993), 73–80. Santiago Martínez had alerted his brothers to the Anglos' plan to summon the troops.

60. Robert W. Larson, *New Mexico's Quest for Statehood, 1846–1912* (Albuquerque: University of New Mexico Press, 1968), 11, 14, 18. The members of the earliest territorial assemblies appear in W. G. Ritch, comp., *The New Mexico Blue Book, 1882* (Santa Fe: Charles W. Greene, 1882), 99ff.

61. See E. K. Francis, "Padre Martínez: A New Mexican Myth," *NMHR* 31 (October 1956):265–89; Ralph H. Vigil, "Willa Cather and Historical Reality," *NMHR* 50 (April 1975):123–34; and many of the essays in *Padre Martínez: New Perspectives*, and Juan Romero, with Moises Sandoval, *Reluctant Dawn: Historia del Padre A. J. Martínez, Cura de Taos* (Los Angeles: Mexican American Cultural Center, 1976).

62. I here follow the probing and balanced interpretation of Chávez, *But Time and Chance*, rather than the sentimentalism of writers such as John Ray de Aragon, "Padre Antonio José Martínez: The Man and the Myth," in *Padre Martínez: New Perspectives*, 125–51.

63. Twitchell, *The History of the Military Occupation*, 134.

64. Thomas J. Steele, "The View from the Rectory," in *Padre Martínez: New Perspectives*, 96.

65. Ritch, *The New Mexico Blue Book*, 101–04.

66. Letters to Pascual Martínez from J. Francisco Chávez, Santa Fe, July 23, 1865, José A. Martínez, August 31, 1865, and Rafael Chacón, September 1, 1865, in PMP, nos. 21, 22, and 99.

67. On August 20, 1851, he received a commission as a brigadier general of the First Brigade of the southern division militia, Territorial Archives of New Mexico, roll 21, frame 42.

68. Antonio José Martínez to Pascual, Taos, January 16, 1855, in PMP, no. 13.

69. Martínez, *The Story of Antonio Severino Martínez*, 12.

70. Tony García of Albuquerque acquired this information in the early 1960s from José Manuel Martínez, a grandson of Pascual, who enjoyed telling of Pascual's trading ventures. José Manuel Martínez possessed some family artifacts as well as stories. Interview with Ward Alan Minge, Corrales, June 16, 1994.

The hacienda today, looking northwest toward the main entry gate.

LA HACIENDA DE LOS MARTÍNEZ

TEXT BY SKIP MILLER
PHOTOGRAPHS BY ANTHONY RICHARDSON

According to undocumented local and family history, a four-room adobe farmstead belonging to Taos Pueblo Indians was already on the tract of land when Severino acquired it, although no structure or reference to existing buildings is recorded in the 1803 deed of purchase for the property. Regardless, Martínez either immediately built living quarters for his family or added on to an existing structure. Within a few years the *casa mayor* consisted of at least the front *placita*, (courtyard) and the surrounding twelve or thirteen rooms.

❖ 1

❖ 2

❖ 3

The great house is constructed of *adobe* (1), a mixture of the local earth, straw, and sand made into sun-dried bricks. The thick walls support massive *vigas*, or beams, which are crossed with a variety of smaller wooden members: *latillas* (2), aspen or cottonwood poles; or *rajas* (3), split cedar or hand-hewn boards. These, in turn, are covered with a layer of grasses, cattails, or rushes and finally topped with up to four feet of mud. This construction technique, first introduced to the Spanish by the Moors sometime in the first millennium B.C., is admirably suited to

Adobe ovens (*hornos*) outside main entryway.

the high, arid Taos Valley, providing comfortable rooms that are relatively warm in the winter and cool in the summer. Remarkably, a similar mud technology was in use by the Pueblo people of the Southwest nearly five hundred years before the arrival of the Spanish. The only significant difference between Spanish and Indian building styles was that the Pueblos used coursed or puddled adobe whereas the Spanish used sun-dried adobe bricks.

Taos in 1804 was at the very northern frontier of the Spanish Empire in the Americas, an area of extreme isolation from the rest of the Spanish world. Spanish pioneers in northern New Mexico were subject to occasional Indian attacks, and life in this remote region was difficult and the environment harsh. In order to survive, frontiersmen had to provide for nearly all of their needs with what they could grow, gather, produce, or manufacture themselves. Independence and self-reliance are still honored characteristics of the Spanish culture of the region.

Precisely these difficult living conditions at the beginning of the nineteenth century caused Severino Martínez to construct his home in a fortress style (4). The high windowless walls, with only massive gates opening to the outside world, pro-

❖ 5

❖ 6

❖ 7

❖ 8

vided the necessary security and protection from Indian attacks. The *pretiles* (5) (parapet walls) were cut with *tronecas* (6) (small gun ports) and constructed high enough to provide cover for the men defending the hacienda. The *zaguans* (7) (double-gate openings) were sufficiently large to allow the great, two-wheeled *caretas* (8) (carts) and some of the livestock to be quickly brought inside in case of attack.

The hacienda was more than just a home for the Martínez family. The *casa mayor* might well have been Taos's first mercantile operation. It functioned in effect as a trading post, general store, and warehouse. This is suggested by the types of materials enumerated in the Severino Martínez will: locally produced agricultural commodities, *efectos del país* (products of the land or country, which included woven and knitted materials), as well as manufactured goods from Mexico and items bartered from Native Americans. Additionally, Severino operated a gristmill and the hacienda became the headquarters for an extensive ranching and farming operation.

The hacienda also may have served in part as an *obraje*, or workshop, where native women captives or servants, most likely under the direct supervision of María del Carmel, processed wool by cleaning, carding, spinning, and then producing finished goods in the form of knitted socks and hats, woven blankets, *sabanilla* (a wool

❖ 9

form of broadcloth or sheeting), *jergas* (rugs), and *serapes* (wearing blankets). They probably made garments and shoes from skins and hides which they had previously tanned and prepared. These native women also would have helped with food preparation, both for immediate consumption and storage, gardening, making soap, watching the children, and a myriad of other domestic chores. They also would have cleaned and maintained the building, including the remudding and replastering of both the interior and exterior walls.

The front placita (9) was a general activity area for the *casa mayor*. Originally it would have had a hard-packed clay surface much like the floors of the interior

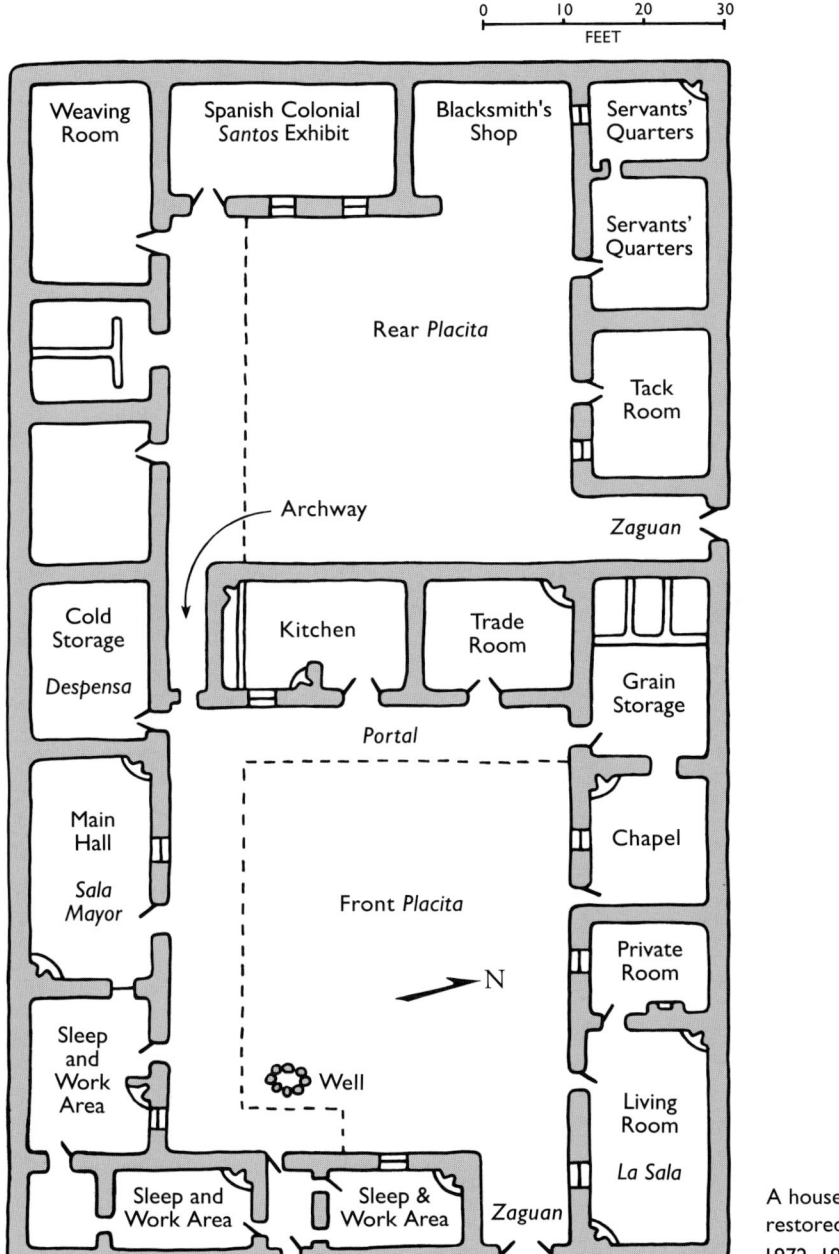

A house restored, 1972–1996.

Pre-restoration views of the hacienda: right, corner fireplace in trade room; below, east wall; far right, storage bins in the *granero*. Photos courtesy Kit Carson Memorial Foundation, Inc.

❖ 12

rooms. Each day, the placita was swept and cleaned. During good weather the women prepared work areas in the placita by spreading out sheepskins to sit on. They would then proceed to card and spin wool or knit socks, process hides, cook, or work at any number of other household tasks.

A vital part of the hacienda was the well *(la noria)*, visible in photo 9. It was located inside the placita for easy access and to assure the family a supply of fresh water should the hacienda suffer an Indian attack.

When the Martínez family first lived here there would have been at least one *horno* (adobe oven) in the placita. The *horno* was used to bake bread, roast fresh corn, and to prepare baked goods ranging from cookies to meats.

The *portal* (porch) (9) that now covers two sides of the placita presumably would have completely surrounded the courtyard, providing a sheltered work area. As many of the rooms originally opened only onto the placita, this allowed the family and servants to stay under cover while going from room to room.

TOURING THE HACIENDA

La sala

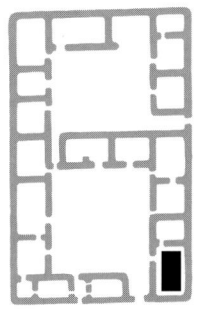

The living room was the primary living area for the Martínez family (13). It would have served as a family room, dining room, classroom, and even bedroom for the family, especially when the children were still young. The family also would have entertained relatives, friends, and visitors in this room.

The size of the hacienda household, which included the large family and numerous servants, would have required great quantities of wood for heating and cooking, especially in the winter. The shallow corner fireplaces were the only sources of heat for the rooms and would have doubled occasionally for cooking. Firewood was gathered in the mountains. As time went on, the forest in and immediately around the plazas in the Taos Valley were depleted. The firewood gatherers and lumbermen, using burros and oxen, had to go greater and greater distances to obtain wood. By the end of the nineteenth century, the distance to the nearest source of wood was probably several miles up into the mountains.

Like most of the floors throughout the hacienda, the floor in this room was composed of a mixture of clayey mud, straw, wood ash, and ox or cattle blood. This mixture provided a hard, durable, waterproof floor that did not give off dust. The surface of the floor could even be polished to a fine gloss by moistening it and burnishing it with a large smooth stone.

As there were no sawmills and iron and tools were extremely scarce, there was little in the way of wooden furniture in the early 1800s. All lumber would have been produced by the labor-intensive process of hand-hewing. Wooden storage boxes, a few simple chairs, and a table would have been the extent of wooden furnishings. There would have been piles of both sheep and buffalo skins, as well as large numbers of woven blankets for sitting, working, and sleeping on and under.

The *cajas* (wooden storage boxes) (14) are superb examples of the six-board style of construction used during the late Spanish Colonial period. The boxes are constructed of hand-hewn, dovetailed ponderosa pine boards and decorated with the beautifully carved rosette patterns and *conchas,* or "shell of the pilgrim," designs.

❖ 14

❖ 15

❖ 16

The *petaca* is a woven leather chest (15) that was probably made in Mexico. This style of container has pre-Columbian origins from the Valley of Mexico. The particular piece here, however, dates to about 1800. It was constructed of buffalo rawhide and decorated with interwoven strips of hide and various colored trade cloth.

The simple daybed or couch in this room (16) would have been a truly extravagant piece of furniture in Severino's day as most people would have slept on skins, blankets, or simple homemade mattresses on the floor. Mattresses of handwoven *sabanilla* stuffed with raw, fluffed wool were common. These were also used as couches by simply leaning a portion against the walls.

The brown-and-white-checkered rugs on the floor are known as *jergas*. This locally produced, simple twill woven material was fabricated on treadle looms from natural, undyed *churro* sheep wool. The same material also was used to make everything from storage bags to clothing. Churro was a major export and trade item both for meat and for skins in the eighteenth and early nineteenth centuries. Churro sheep, raised in New Mexico, yielded three times the amount of wool compared to those from New Spain. The demand for them and their wool grew so much that in August 1800 an unscheduled caravan was sent south, delivering more than 200 cattle and nearly 19,000 churros along with pelts and wool.

There were few luxuries available to Severino and María del Carmel Martínez, and most of these probably came later in their lives. Exceptions are pieces of the bright and colorful Puebla-style pottery from Mexico and the beautiful cashmere *rebosas* (shawls) that were made in the Philippines and brought up from Mexico via the yearly trade caravans.

After 1821, many different materials, especially woven cotton fabrics, were available from the *norteamericanos* through the Santa Fe Trail. Severino's will lists among his personal luxury possessions a saber with a silver scabbard, a large gilded mirror, a silver cup, and four settings of silver plates, spoons, and forks—not much by today's standards for the man who in 1827 was considered to be the wealthiest and most influential in the Taos area.

Little is known about the day-to-day activities of frontier Spanish families during this time period, but it is safe to assume that everyone, even the children, worked hard. Survival was dependent on every member of the family participating to the fullest of his or her capabilities, regardless of age.

The family is extremely important to the Hispanic culture of northern New Mexico. Many customs existed in the culture that established and secured extensive relationships both within and beyond the family. A complex structure of reciprocal relations and obligations provided for the kind of support and assistance necessary for sustaining life on the frontier. The Catholic church and the true faith of the people helped both to establish and formalize these bonds through such rituals and associated celebrations as baptism, confirmation, and marriage. This array of customs and support also helped maintain a spiritual connection to an ever more distant Spanish homeland and heritage.

La recamara

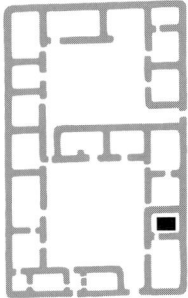

This room may have been the bedroom but more likely was a private area for Severino and María del Carmel in their later years (17). A small altar with images of Christ, various personal saints, and tallow candles would have been an important feature in the room. The altar table is covered with a beautiful example of *colcha*, a regional style of long-stitch embroidery. The shape and design of the fireplace in this room is unique, but there is no way to determine if this was the original or a later period adaptation.

In the early days of Spanish colonization, tallow candles were virtually the only available source of safe interior lighting. These candles were especially important for the family altars (18) and *capillas* (chapels). Originally, tallow was made from the rendered hard fat of buffalo. It was an essential trade item obtained from the Plains Indians or Pueblo or Spanish buffalo hunting expeditions on the plains east of the Sangre de Cristo Mountains.

La capilla

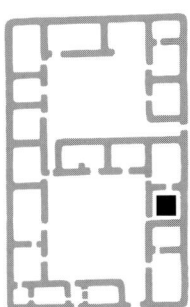

It was common for wealthier families in Spanish Colonial New Mexico to set aside a room as a chapel. There the family would gather for daily prayer, and visiting priests would say Mass or perform other religious rituals to benefit the household. The chapel would have had a small altar and possibly a *reredo* (altar screen) and a number of *santos* (religious images). The room also might have had a few simple *bancos* (benches) to seat people while at prayer or attending a service.

Although there is no documentary evidence that this room was ever used as a chapel in Severino's time, the ornate corbels supporting the roof beams suggest the importance of the room.

El granero y la despensa

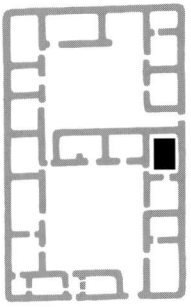

Wheat, barley, and corn were important agricultural products of the Taos Valley. The large adobe bins in this room were used for storage (19). Grain produced by local farmers was used to barter for the manufactured goods that Severino brought up from Mexico or, after 1821, acquired from the merchants on the Santa Fe Trail.

❖ 17

❖ 18

❖ 19

❖ 20

Wheat and barley, introduced to New Mexico by the Spanish, grew very well in the high, cool Taos Valley. Taos was such an ideal location for growing wheat that during Severino's lifetime it was considered the "breadbasket" of New Mexico. Barley appears to have been used primarily for animal feed rather than for human consumption. Varieties of native and hybridized corn were grown widely in New Mexico, although only marginally at 7000 feet in the Taos area.

All grains and other dry goods were measured by standard units of volume: *la fanega* and *el almud*. A *fanega* is roughly equivalent to a bushel, or approximately one hundred pounds of grain. The *almud* (20), a word derived directly from Arabic, was determined as one-twelfth of a *fanega*. Uniform, scooplike boxes were constructed to provide consistent measurement for the grain and produce traded at the hacienda.

Other foodstuff, such as garlic, onions, and root crops, was stored in straw- or sand-filled adobe bins, small root cellars, or simple pits covered with straw. Severino's will indicates that he owned a water-powered gristmill, believed to have been located just to the east of the front *zaguan*.

Cuarto de cambalache

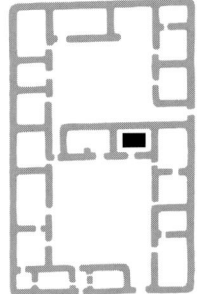

The trade room (21) demonstrates the great variety of items bartered, bought, or sold at the hacienda. Manufactured goods from Mexico, large quantities of locally produced woolen goods, and skins and hides obtained through trade with Spanish and Pueblo and Plains Indian trappers were among those items.

❖ 21

La cocina

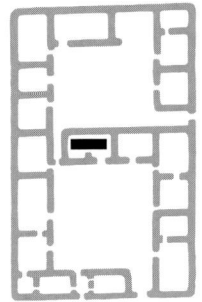

The spacious kitchen (22) was probably a constant hive of activity and strictly the domain of the women. Much if not all of the food necessary to support the family and workers of the hacienda was prepared in a kitchen similar to this one. By the early part of the nineteenth century there was an adequate food supply for even the poorest of Spanish families in the Taos Valley. Most raised at least some sheep, pigs, or chickens, and family gardens provided many vegetables, which could be stored

❖ 22

or preserved for winter use. Wild game and fish also were abundant in the rivers, mountains, and hills surrounding Taos.

When the Spanish came to the area, the Pueblos were using a variety of domestic and wild plants—fruits, leaves, seeds, and roots—for food and medicinal purposes. The Spanish introduced apricot, cherry, apple, peach, pear, quince, domestic plum, and grapes to supplement local resources. Garden crops included lettuce, squash, radishes, cabbages, onions, melons, pumpkins, beets, horsebeans, and a variety of dried beans and peas. The kitchen also was a storeroom for the dried vegetables, herbs, and spices needed for both cooking and medicine.

The *fogon de pastor* (shepherd's hearth or bed) provided a warm resting or sleeping area for the children, the elderly, or sick members of the household. It also functioned as a large "stove" with nearly fifteen feet of cooking space. A large fire was kept burning in the chamber. From there, coals could be scooped out and

❖ 23

placed anywhere along the hearth where pots, caldrons, or griddles could be placed to heat. The smoke and fumes would be drawn up and along under the large hand-hewn beam and pulled up the flue at the fireplace end.

The large six-board *harinero* (grain chest) (23) is an extraordinary piece of work. Each panel of the chest is a single, hand-hewn board dovetailed to the adjoining boards. The reinforcing iron and the hinges were probably added sometime between 1850 and 1900. Such chests were made to store grains and flour and were fashioned to be reasonably vermin-proof.

La despensa

Like many of the rooms in the hacienda, the *despensa* (cold room) (24) probably was used for many different purposes over the years. In Severino's time, storage was an important function of the *casa mayor*. A cold room might be set aside for

✧ 24

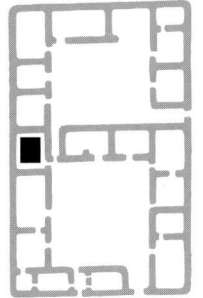

the storage of all manner of fruits, vegetables, and even meat. The unheated room essentially functioned as a refrigerator, maintaining very cool temperatures in summer and cold— but protection from freezing— in winter. A small, shuttered window placed near the ceiling drew out warm air, and a small door used only when stocking or removing goods allowed the room to remain cold.

LA SALA MAYOR

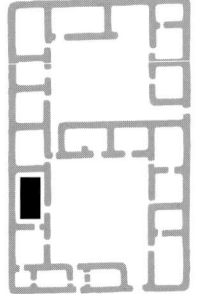

The *sala mayor,* or main hall (25), is the largest room in the hacienda and the only room in the house with a wooden floor. The rough, hand-hewn planks represent a major effort in both time and labor. Because of the scarcity of iron and woodworking tools, finished wood of any kind during the early years of the nineteenth century was extremely valuable. Thus, the floor in the *sala mayor* is indicative both of the growing wealth and importance of the Martínez family.

Severino Martínez provided this room for the use of the local community as well as for his own needs. The room was large enough for all types of events: religious meetings, social and political gatherings, parties, and *fandangos* (dances). When not in use for social events, the room could have been used

for storage, to provide shelter for travelers and traders, as a workplace for the hacienda servants, or even as a play area for children during periods of bad weather.

The interior walls of this room, like many throughout the hacienda, are finished with *tierra blanca*. The local white mica clay was blended with a cooked wheat paste and applied to the adobe plaster on the walls. This glittering surface helped to brighten rooms by reflecting light from the myriad mica flecks. Taos folklore says that children liked the taste of the mixture and would often lick the walls.

As Severino's wealth increased through his many business and ranching ventures, he gained political power as well. Church records indicate that Severino and María del Carmel sponsored many baptisms. Through the sponsorship of such ceremonies and celebrations, the families of the children became obligated to the Martínez family. Likewise, Severino and María del Carmel would have had the responsibility of adopting and rearing these children as their own should anything happen to the parents. In this way, Severino was able to share his wealth and extend his influence while securing a position of authority within the community.

OTHER ROOMS, PLACITA DE ENFRENTE

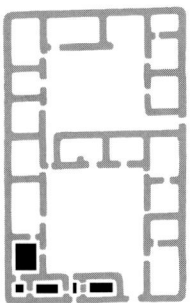

The rooms that include the present reception area and utility rooms were probably used by Severino and María del Carmel's children as bedrooms and work areas as they grew to adulthood. In 1813, following the death of his young bride, José Antonio Martínez returned from Abiquiú to live in his father's house until he made the decision to enter the priesthood in 1817. Possibly two or all three of Padre Martínez's brothers also lived in their father's house as adults. The youngest son, Pascual Bailon, had not married at the time of his father's death. He inherited or acquired the hacienda after his mother's death in 1829 and so had most likely always lived in the house of his birth.

PLACITA DE ATRÁS

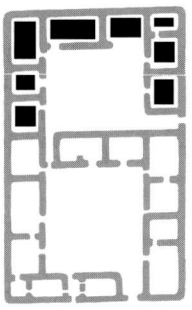

In 1972, when the Museums acquired the hacienda, only a stub of wall remained of the original rear placita. Following archaeological investigations, the remains of the exterior wall as well as the foundations were located, which tentatively defined a few enclosed rooms and a fireplace. However, the remaining rooms or stable areas are conjecture. The back placita would have served primarily as a stable, with a tack room for horses and oxen. Additional storage may have been a component of the rear placita. There also would have been housing for captives or servants and possibly workrooms for weaving or knitting.

Today the back placita offers the visitor an opportunity to see and experience some of the living traditions of those early Hispanic settlers. Many of the arts of

❖ 26

Spanish Colonial New Mexico are still being practiced today and are demonstrated at the hacienda.

The beautiful archway (26) that connects the front and rear placitas was constructed entirely of adobe without additional wooden support. This architectural detail is a rare survivor of late Spanish Colonial building technology. The passageway was used to hang and cure meats during the cold fall and winter months.

❖ 27

Pieza de Tejer

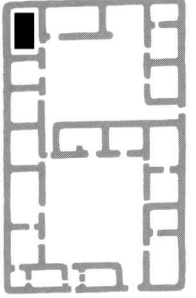

Spinning, weaving, and knitting were extremely important economic activities in New Mexico from the beginning of the Spanish Colonial period until the first part of the twentieth century (27). For nearly three hundred years locally woven textiles provided for most of the clothing needs of northern New Mexicans and were a vital source of trade for manufactured goods. Today, traditional Hispanic textiles from northern New Mexico are valued and collected internationally.

Santos from the collection

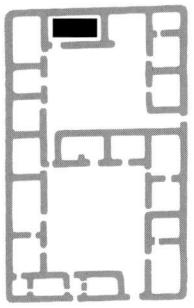

Although the Martínez family had *santos* (religious images of saints) in their home, none were listed in Severino's will. The religious art of northern New Mexico flourished in the late eighteenth and early nineteenth centuries as the Spanish colony expanded. Severino and María del Carmel would have arrived in Taos at the height of the *santero* (saint-maker) period (28).

Today the art is flourishing in New Mexico, with numerous talented new carvers and painters inspired by the old styles but seeking their own individual expression.

❖ 29

Herrería

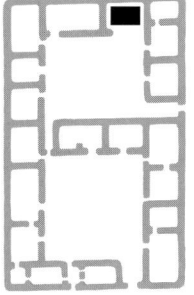

According to the materials listed in the will, there does not appear to have been a blacksmith shop (29) in the hacienda at the time of Severino's death. Iron was extremely scarce on the remote frontier of northern New Mexico. Virtually all the raw material in the form of iron bars had to come from Spain via Mexico. Therefore, because of its scarcity and value, every single pound of it was accounted for in the probate of the will. Numerous iron farm implements, including hoes, axes, and scythes, were listed, as well as an iron grate, beaver traps, a saw, an iron spindle, two cranks, a shovel, a scale with weights, several wedges, and a branding iron. Four *trabucos* (blunderbusses) and three *fusiles* (muskets) were also listed as part of the estate. Iron household items were limited to several locks and hinges mounted to doors. Due to the omission of hammers, tongs, anvils, or other ironworking tools, it is unlikely that Severino had a blacksmith shop in his hacienda. However, his youngest son, Pascual, was known to have had a large herd of horses. He may have added a blacksmith shop to the *casa mayor* after his father's death.

Cuartos de los captivos

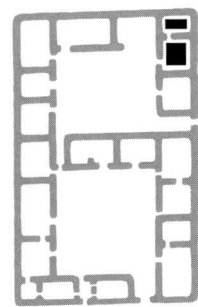

The use of slaves was a common practice throughout the world during the colonial period (30). Prior to the European conquest of the New World, indigenous peoples of the Americas also kept slaves.

There is strong, primarily circumstantial evidence that the Martínez family owned a number of Native American captives. Severino's will listed bequests of substantial pieces of property to two of his former servants—both thought to have been Indian captives. Additional evidence for slave owning is revealed through historic documents from 1818 that substantiate Severino's involvement in a legal dispute over the ownership of a mule that had been exchanged for a young Ute women.

Since the beginning of Spanish colonization in the Southwest, the forced taking and using of Native Americans contributed significantly to the economy of the region. Taos was one of the major centers for the trafficking and distribution of Indian captives from slave raids, the vast majority of which were Navajo, Apache, or Ute women and children. These captives provided the primary labor needed to operate the mines, to maintain the growing herds of sheep and cattle, to produce leather and woolen goods, and to furnish Hispanic households with domestic servants.

Cuarto de tachuela

At the end of his life, Severino Martínez owned more than sixty horses, twenty-eight mules, nine burros, and forty-one oxen. His will lists the animals along with a substantial quantity of both riding and pack saddles, saddlebags, ropes, and other items of tack. These items would probably have been stored in a room or enclosure in the rear placita and corral area.

❖ 30

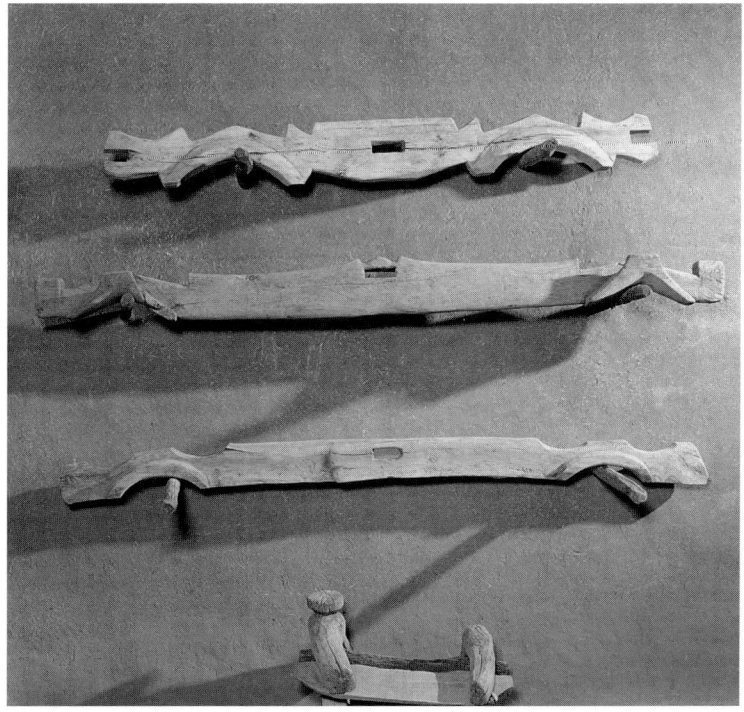

❖ 31

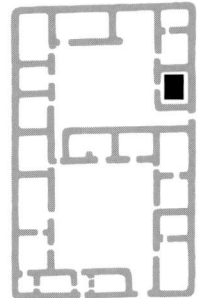

The hand-carved ox-horn yokes (31) are superb examples of Spanish Colonial craftsmanship and practical application. Oxen were an important part of both farming and trade at the hacienda, as well as a source of meat. These gentle but powerful creatures plowed the fields and pulled the massive two-wheeled carts that were used for transporting large quantities of goods. By about 1800, the *carretas* were being replaced by pack animals for long-distance hauling, but their use in local commerce continued into the beginning of the twentieth century. When an ox was slaughtered for meat, the blood was mixed with clay and straw to make the floors in many homes.

Today the tack room serves as a demonstration area for Spanish Colonial furniture making, still an important craft in northern New Mexico. Although the advent of modern tools and milled lumber has made the process easier, many craftspeople still do the intricate carving and joinery by hand using traditional tools.

Utility rooms

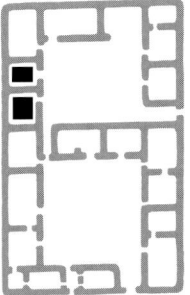

Originally, the rooms that currently serve as utility and public rest rooms may have been simply roofed stalls for animals, enclosed storage, work areas, or additional servants' quarters. The archaeological investigations of the rear placita did not identify any interior wall foundations or features such as fireplaces for this area. Only the exterior wall was defined by stone and adobe foundation outlines.

Little is documented about how people dealt with the disposal of human waste during the Spanish and even Mexican

The Martínez Hacienda in 1903, photographed by Taos painter E. Irving Couse, who rented studio space in the *casa mayor's* north side. Photos courtesy Couse Family Archives, Couse Enterprises, Ltd.

periods in northern New Mexico. From the scanty evidence that has survived, it must be concluded that chamber pots were the primary form of in-home disposal—a practice common to the Pueblos dating back into prehistoric times.

Despite the best attempts by the women of the household to maintain some degree of cleanliness, the extremely difficult conditions of frontier life resulted in high rates of infant mortality. Deaths were caused by gastrointestinal illnesses such as diarrhea and the resulting dehydration and by anemia and respiratory disorders. Bedbugs, lice, fleas, and other vermin also were commonplace. Bathing was not a common practice in provincial New Mexico until the latter part of the nineteenth century. As a consequence of the generally poor hygiene and living conditions and lack of proper medicines, communicable disease such as colds, influenza, measles, and smallpox spread rapidly through families and small communities, often with devastating effects.

CHAPTER
❖ EIGHT

THE ASA MAYOR

THE LEGACY OF SEVERINO MARTÍNEZ included his half of the main residence on the Río del Pueblo, what his descendants called the *casa mayor*.[1] By the time of his death, the one-story, flat-roofed adobe house appears to have consisted of thirteen rooms arranged around a central courtyard, or *placita*, ringed by a covered porch, known in New Mexico as a *portal*.[2] If, as family tradition holds, Severino and María had purchased a four-room house at the site [3] then they had more than tripled the number of rooms. They had also built a house three to four times larger than the average Hispanic house in New Mexico of their day, whose rooms generally numbered three or four.[4]

THE NEW MEXICO MANOR HOUSE

A fortress as well as a house, the exterior walls (90' x 100') of the Martínez *casa mayor* presented a solid face to the outside world. Almost all windows and doors looked inward to the *placita*. Only three opened to the outside—an eleven-foot-wide, two-door gateway at the front of the house, which permitted wagons and animals to enter the central courtyard, and two small doorways, one on the front of the house and another that led to a second walled courtyard, measuring ninety feet by sixty feet, which was used as a corral. The structure had fire walls, or *pretiles*—a standard feature of New Mexican structures of that day—and perhaps, as family tradition suggests, they were notched with loopholes (*tronecas*) and high enough to protect men stationed on the roof during attack.[5]

Defensive features, however, did not set the Martínez's house apart from other great houses in New Mexico. "All the larger buildings have more the appearance of so many diminutive fortifications, than of private residences," Josiah Gregg wrote in 1844. The Martínez house fit the pattern described by Gregg:

> *A tier of rooms on each side of a square . . . encompass an open* patio *or court, with but one door opening into the street—a huge gate, called* la puerta del zaguan. *The back tier is generally occupied with the* cocina, dispensa [despensa], granero *(kitchen, provision-store, and granary), and other offices of the same kind.*[6]

Like many New Mexican structures, the Martínez house also seems to have had an attached corral for livestock. That style of rural dwelling, commonplace in New Mexico, has been aptly termed a "casa-corral." Whether Severino had also built service buildings inside the walls of his corral (as we see today) or whether those rooms were added later is not clear. When the attached corral began to resemble a second courtyard, the house itself probably came to seem more grand and so be understood as a manor house—a *casa de hacienda*.[7]

What set the Martínez's house apart from the manor houses occupied by many of their contemporaries was less its form or its size than the fact that one family occupied the entire house. Some structures that appeared from the outside to be manor houses were most likely the dwellings of multiple families who had built rooms contiguously around a central courtyard for defense. Such multiple family homes were not unusual in New Mexico.[8]

Romantic writers have supposed that families such as the Martínezes lived in gracious, two-story houses built around central courtyards, with "*salas* for dancing."[9] Two-story adobes were a rarity, though, in Spanish or Mexican New Mexico.[10] By the standards of *hacendados* in more prosperous areas of the

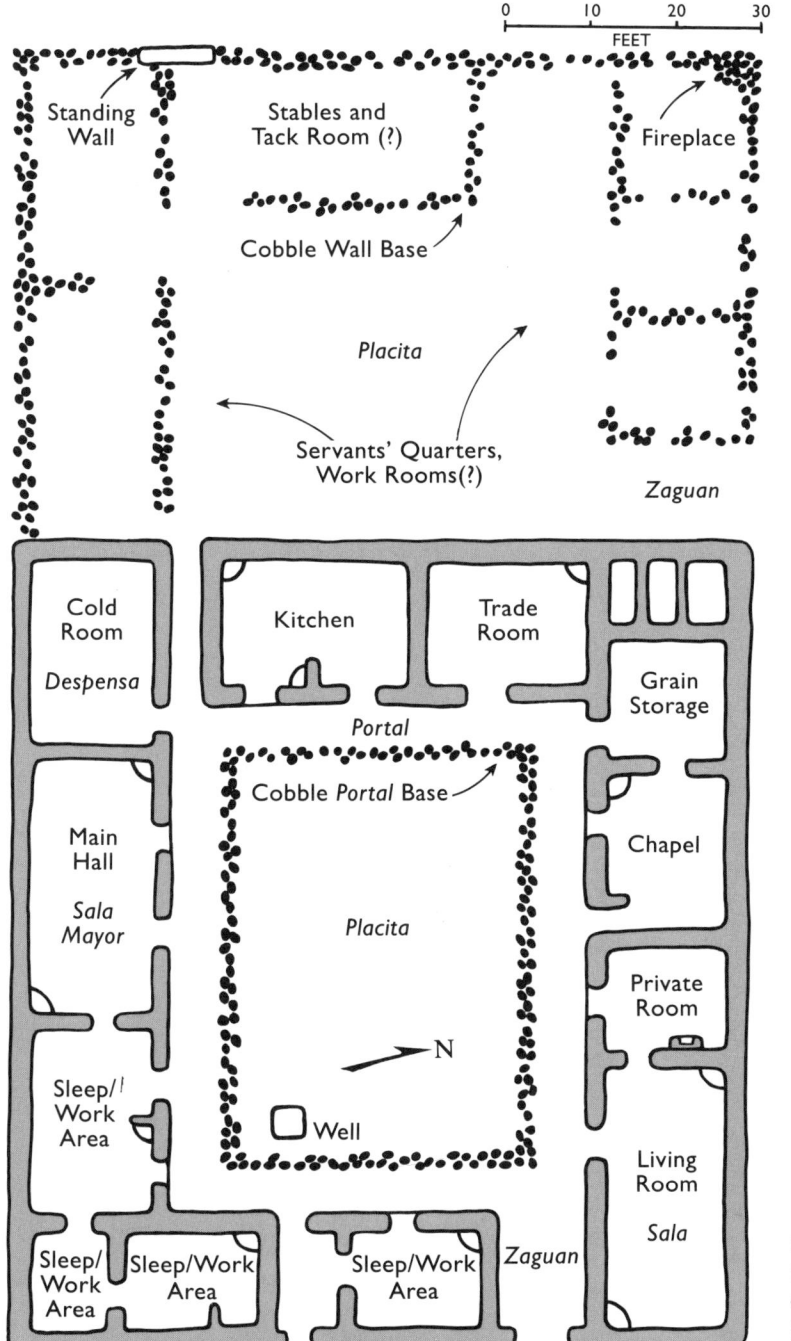

Original foundations and exterior walls (1972 Excavation).

Spanish Empire, the interiors of most of New Mexico's *casas de hacienda* would have seemed mean and sparse.

Although the executors of don Severino's estate identified many objects in the house, including a gilded mirror, they made little mention of furniture. Instead they listed many cloth items, including carpets (*jergas* and *alfombras*), mattresses, and pillows.[11] Like other well-off New Mexicans, they probably covered their hard-packed earthen floors with carpet and lined the whitewashed walls of their room with calico "to the height of five or six feet" to prevent the whitewash from rubbing off on their clothes.[12]

As numerous visitors attested, New Mexicans placed little movable furniture in those cloth-lined rooms, and what tables and chairs they had they often preferred not to use, "the prevailing fashion," Josiah Gregg noted, "being to fold mattresses against the walls, which, being covered over with blankets, are thus converted into sofas."[13] As late as 1848, a visitor to Taos described the practice of rolling blankets or serapes against the walls of the rooms, where they served as "beds by night and lounges by day."[14] New Mexicans' ability to do fine carpentry was limited by the shortage of iron tools and of iron itself for latches and hinges.[15] Hence, the heirs of Severino Martínez placed a value on windows, doors, and locks in his portion of the house.[16]

New Mexicans did, however, use immovable furniture—built-in wooden cabinets, adobe benches, adobe fireplaces—and they decorated their walls with religious objects. At Embudo, south of Taos, Albert Pike entered the winter room of such a house in December 1831:

❖

In one corner of it stood the little fireplace, like a square stove, open on two sides, and filled with small sticks of pine set upright and burning, filling the room with all heat and comfort. Round the whole room, except the part occupied by two mattrasses [sic], was a pile of blankets, striped red and white, answering the purpose of sofas. High up on the walls were various small looking-glasses, pictures of saints, wooden images of the Saviour, and wooden crucifixes interspersed with divers roses of red and white cambric. These, with two or three wooden benches which served for both chairs and tables, completed the furniture of the room.[17]

The parlor, or *sala*, in the house that Pike visited was not used for dancing that December. While the family crowded into their smaller winter room, the unheated *sala* had been converted to a storeroom, "garnished with vast quantities of buffalo meat, in thin, dry fleeces, as well as with huge strings of onions, and of red and green pepper, besides numberless saddle-trees, heavy bridles, and not a few buffalo robes."[18]

THE HOUSE DIVIDED

Comfortable and functional, if not gracious or opulent, don Severino's fortlike house passed on to his heirs according to the terms of his will. In the fashion of the day, he had divided his portion of the house among them room by room.[19] His widow, who, it appears, already owned several rooms in the house on her own account, received two rooms with plank roofs, one of them described as small. Together, they measured thirteen and a half varas in length. She also received the "little room with a basement and with a small portal and picket fence" and a four-vara length of the portal of the living room, or *sala*.[20]

Three of Severino's sons received other parts of the house—his two daughters and the priest, Antonio José, apparently did not wish to live in or own part of the old homestead.[21] To José María de Jesús went the plank-floored main hall (the "*sala mayor*") measuring sixteen varas, nine varas of the portal of the main hall (of which his mother had an additional four varas), and the ten-vara pantry ("*despensa*") contiguous to the main hall. To José Santiago went a windowless partitioned storeroom, fifteen varas in length, and an adjoining room, nine and a half varas long, which ended at the *zaguan*, or main gate. Finally, to the youngest son, Juan Pascual, went "one small room made of boards with its little hall, which adjoins the room of our mother to the passageway [or] zaguan."[22]

As the will of Severino Martínez suggests, New Mexicans measured and appraised their rooms by length rather than by length and width; widths tended to be standard, limited by the lengths of the beams, or *vigas*, that supported the roof. Plank flooring or roofing made a room more valuable—one peso and six reales per vara as opposed to a peso per vara for a room with the usual dirt floor or ceiling of sticks (*latillas*). The value of a room depended, too, on its condition and on the number of wooden doors, window frames, and metal door locks. Those items, generally appraised at a peso each in don Severino's estate, were itemized separately.

With the passage of time, all of the house, together with nearby land, outlying buildings, and mill, passed into the hands of don Severino's youngest son, Pascual. There, in the *casa mayor*, Pascual and his wife, Teodora Gallegos y Lucero of Abiquiú, raised eight children.[23] Although Pascual and his wife did

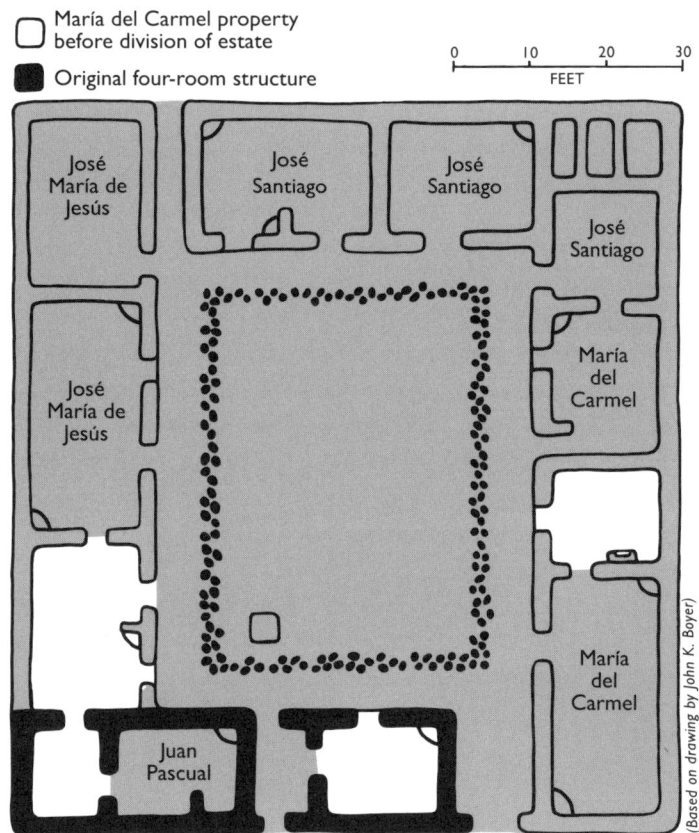

The house divided, 1827.

extensive remodeling—adding eleven exterior windows, two doorways, and an exterior portal across the facade—they apparently saw no need to enlarge the spacious house.[24] When Pascual died in 1882 the house passed on to his heirs. It still contained thirteen rooms, plus adjoining corral and barns, and was appraised that year at $400.[25] For several generations thereafter it continued to be remembered as the Pascual Martínez house, although some writers mistakenly imagined it to be the house of Padre Antonio José Martínez.[26]

Members of the Martínez family lived in the house until 1931, when Virginia Martínez, the widow of Pascual's son Agapito, sold the property to Desmond O'Ryan and his wife, Leona Read, the daughter of the historian Benjamin Read, for a recorded sum of $10.[27] Although she lived abroad, Leona

Read purchased and maintained the estate in the hope that it might become a museum. In the words of a writer who knew her then:

> *she wishes to preserve it and keep its precious heritage for posterity that they may know how the families of colonial Spain conducted their homes. . . . No more fitting use could be found for the historic manor than to make it a treasure trove to house the valuable collections of authentic mementos of colonial days that are left in the community.*[28]

Leona Read owned the property as late as 1940 and may still have owned it when Taos artist Martin Shaeffer reportedly lived in the house and restored parts of it in 1944. At some point, perhaps after World War II, the house reverted to the Martínez family. Public records show that Fares Elías Martínez and his wife, Julia, owned the house in 1964, although they apparently did not live in it. Fares Martínez was the great-grandson of Severino Martínez, the grandson of Pascual Martínez, and the son of Agapito Martínez y Gallegos and Virginia Gonzales.[29]

After World War II, if not earlier, the house began to fall into disrepair. In 1960, architectural historian Bainbridge Bunting vividly described the forces of decay:

> *Because of leaking roofs, pools of water collected in certain rooms, weakening foundations, and causing the walls to sag. Most destructive of all, treasure hunters ransacked the abandoned house. They excavated under every fireplace and in almost every corner. Then groundhogs began undermining the never-too-sturdy foundations. Vandals broke window sash and wind tore off shutters.*[30]

It seemed to Bunting that by 1960 "the house had probably deteriorated beyond the point of redemption," as had eleven of the twelve structures that he described in his book *Taos Adobes* (1964). Of those dozen houses, only the Martínez house remained after the mid-1970s, thanks to the intercession of new owners.[31]

The House Preserved

In early 1964 Jerome and Anne Milford bought the empty Martínez house, together with 1,456 acres around it, from Fares and Julia Martínez.[32] That summer the Milfords began extensive renovation. They replaced eroded adobes, built new roofing, added cement footing and cement-and-steel capping around the perimeter of much of the structure, and tore down and replaced some 140 feet of wall.[33] Unfortunately, they never completed the work; the couple divorced in 1969. Jerome Milford continued to pay taxes on the property until 1972. That year he sold the house and three and a half acres surrounding it to the Kit Carson Memorial Foundation, which administered the Kit Carson Home and Museum in Taos.[34]

Under the leadership of its director, Jack K. Boyer, the Kit Carson Memorial Foundation began to breathe life back into the dying house—what Boyer had come to call "La Hacienda de Don Antonio Severino Martínez." Boyer's dream was to restore and furnish the much-modified *casa mayor* "as when occupied by Don Antonio [Severino] and his family." The foundation would then open it to the public to depict the late Spanish Colonial period in Taos.[35]

Boyer succeeded in having the site included on the National Register of Historic Places in the spring of 1973.[36] At the same time, he consulted with specialists, such as Bainbridge Bunting and Ward Alan Minge, and drew reminiscences from descendants of Severino Martínez. At the foundation's invitation, some 250 of his descendants met in Taos on April 14, 1973, many of them offering support, advice, and memories.[37]

A plan formulated, the foundation began restoration work in the winter of 1974–75, with donated adobes and vigas. That first winter the crew consisted entirely of Boyer, his curator Jack Dyson, and the foundation's maintenance man.[38] Restoration began on a shoestring.

Boyer soon proved himself a master at marshaling resources by appealing to the generosity of the Taos community, working with government agencies, submitting to the review of the New Mexico State Preservation Officer, and attempting to follow the U.S. Secretary of the Interior's Standards for Historic Preservation Projects. Federal aid enabled Boyer to halt further deterioration of the base of the old adobe walls. Built without benefit of a foundation, the mud walls lifted water from the ground like a wick in oil. With Boyer's prodding, the U.S. Soil Conservation Service created a drainage system to lower the water table around the house—a task they completed in 1978.

Meanwhile, Boyer had also acquired more manpower—crews working under a federal program, the Comprehensive Employment and Training Act (CETA). From 1977 through 1981, when the U.S. Congress discontinued the program, the CETA workers enabled the foundation to make steady progress. They built adobes, erected new walls on the old foundations, plastered and painted walls inside and out, poured and finished mud flooring, built fireplaces, adzed planks for the one room with a wood floor, cut aspen, cedar, and spruce in the high country and painstakingly stripped the bark or split the saplings for the ceilings, and cut and installed cedar posts for fencing. More skilled workers, some on staff and some donating their time, did finishing work—adzing windows and doors and hinging them with *pinteles* as they might have done two centuries before. The staff blacksmith made hinges for the zaguan and door pulls and latches for other doors. Archaeological investigation, begun in 1975, informed some of the restoration, as did the invaluable will of don Severino.[39]

The Kit Carson Memorial Foundation did not, and perhaps never will, possess enough information to restore the house *exactly* as Severino Martínez built it, but Boyer did the best restoration possible with the information and resources at his disposal.[40] Although he could not turn the clock back, his work provides a setting that encourages visitors to imagine themselves back in time: when water came from the well in the courtyard; when a ladder stood ready to facilitate repair of the thick dirt roof; when metal was scarce and doors and windows opened on wooden pegs or pintels; when hand-packed mud covered floors and mud plaster covered walls; when windows of selenite substituted for glass; when fireplaces provided the only heat in winter rooms; when self-sufficiency was a necessity; and when family members and servants raised animals and crops, prepared and stored foods for the winter, and made soap, candles, cloth, and clothing.

On October 8–9, 1983, ten years and $500,000 after it acquired the property, the Kit Carson Memorial Foundation formally dedicated the restored Martínez house in a weekend celebration. The ceremonies included a second gathering of descendants of Antonio Severino and María del Carmel Martínez and the blessing of the house by the Rev. Albert Schneider of Our Lady of Guadalupe Church in Taos. Responding to the stories that the house was haunted, Father Schneider said, "May the ghosts in this place be a little holier and less lively after the blessing of this house."[41]

The Kit Carson Memorial Foundation's ambitious work of bringing the house and times of don Severino back to life included the reconstruction of log storage buildings that may have stood near the rear wall of the great house in his day; using hand axes and time-honored techniques, Tomás García and Art Leach completed that work in 1986.[42] The foundation plans to reconstruct Severino's mill, which apparently stood on the river in front of the house.[43]

Since the mid-1980s, the Martínez hacienda has attracted attention in national as well as local media.[44] Published guides to the Taos area recommend it, together with the Ernest Blumenschein and Kit Carson historic houses, as one of the three museums that depict the region's history.[45] That favorable publicity, combined with the steady growth of tourism in Taos, has made the hacienda a popular destination for thousands of visitors every year.[46]

Coming from an increasingly urbanized America, many of those visitors have been charmed by the rusticity of rural Taos. However harsh life may have been for the Martínez clan in early-nineteenth-century Taos, modern-day visitors have found it a bucolic place. The sentiments of a Kansas writer, Nobel Prentis, expressed eloquently on a visit to Santa Fe in the early 1880s, echo yet today in Taos:

> *If I was dyspeptic, worn out, a-weary of the world, tired of living and yet afraid of dying, I should come to Santa Fe in the summertime and take some big, high, white-washed rooms in a Mexican house, with a fireplace in the corner; and with books at home and a horse to ride abroad, I believe I could find a new body and a fresh soul. I would . . . do nothing with great care and elaboration for awhile, and then I would return to the United States and join the "march of progress," which is doubtless a great thing, but which makes many people footsore.*[47]

Notes

1. In executing Severino's estate, his sons Antonio José and Santiago referred to the house as the "*casa mayor* on the plaza of San Francisco del Ranchito." Ward Alan Minge, ed. and trans., "The Last Will and Testament of Don Severino Martínez," *New Mexico Quarterly* 33 (Spring 1963):50 (see the Spanish-language original). "*Casa mayor*" implies the main house or the ancestral house rather than the "big house" or "large house," which would be a *casa grande*.

2. Jack K. Boyer, who analyzed the will of Severino Martínez and directed the reconstruction of the house, concluded that it had thirteen rooms by 1827. He finds mention of nine rooms in the will and judges that four rooms belonged to María del Carmel and were not mentioned in the will: "rooms 2, 9, 10, and 13 belonged to the mother as her share of the home before division of the estate [and] hence are not mentioned in the Will." Boyer to Myra Ellen Jenkins, Taos, July 15, 1978.

Collection of the Cultural Properties Review Committee, SRCA, courtesy of Richard Salazar. Severino's will is susceptible to different interpretations.

3. The deed of sale from Antonio Archuleta to Severino Martín mentions only land, not structure. Deed Records of Taos County, New Mexico, vol. A–20, p. 546, filed in 1911. Translation in Northern New Mexico Abstract and Title Company, Taos, New Mexico, Abstract of Title, no. A–597. Xerox copies of both Spanish transcription and English translation in KCHM.

4. Frances Levine, "Hispanic Household Structure in Colonial New Mexico," in Bradley J. Vierra and Clara Gualtieri, eds., *Current Research on the Late Prehistory and Early History of New Mexico* (Albuquerque: New Mexico Archaeological Council Special Publication 1, July 1992), 205. E. Boyd, *Popular Arts of Spanish New Mexico* (Santa Fe: Museum of New Mexico Press, 1974), 7.

5. Bainbridge Bunting, *Taos Adobes: Spanish Colonial and Territorial Architecture of the Taos Valley* (Santa Fe: Fort Burgwin Research Center and Museum of New Mexico Press, 1964), 24; National Register of Historic Places, nomination form, entry number NR 4–23–73, prepared by James Purdy, archivist, SRCA, November 2, 1972, Collection of the Cultural Properties Review Committee, State of New Mexico, in SRCA; and Philip Riley Bartholomew, "The Hacienda: Its Evolvement and Architecture in Colonial New Mexico, 1598–1821" (Ph.D. diss., University of Missouri, Columbia, 1983), 170–97, a deeply flawed work that contains a discussion of the Martínez house based in part on conversations with Jack Boyer.

6. Josiah Gregg, *Commerce of the Prairies*, Max L. Moorhead, ed. (1st ed., 1844; Norman: University of Oklahoma Press, 1954), 144–45. See, too, W. W. H. Davis, *El Gringo: or, New Mexico and Her People* (1st ed., 1857; Santa Fe: Rydal Press, 1938), 40: "The almost universal style of building, both in town and country, is in the form of a square, with a court-yard in the center."

7. Marc Simmons, "Settlement Patterns and Village Plans in New Mexico," in David J. Weber, ed., *New Spain's Far Northern Frontier: Essays on Spain in the American West, 1540–1821* (Albuquerque: University of New Mexico Press, 1979), 107. The custom of building a *casa grande* around a central courtyard certainly had Iberian antecedents but was not followed uniformly. In south Texas in that era, for example, ranchers built their houses in the form of simple massive cubes. Willard B. Robinson, "Colonial Ranch Architecture in the Spanish-Mexican Tradition," *Southwestern Historical Quarterly* 83 (October 1979):123–50.

8. Nancy L. González, *The Spanish-Americans of New Mexico: A Heritage of Pride* (Albuquerque: University of New Mexico Press, 1967), 35.

9. Mary Austin, "Mexicans and New Mexico," *Survey* 66 (1931), 142, quoted in González, *The Spanish-Americans*, 34–35.

10. Davis, *El Gringo*, 40, reported that only two could be found in Santa Fe in the early 1850s, both built by foreigners; and Boyd, *Popular Arts*, 26.

11. Minge, "Last Will and Testament," 53, mentions all of these items, including some stools, tables, boxes, and a cabinet.

12. Gregg, *Commerce of the Prairies*, 145–46.

13. Ibid., 146.

14. George Douglas Brewerton, *Overland with Kit Carson: A Narrative of the Old Spanish Trial in 48*, Stallo Vinton, ed. (New York: Coward-McCann, 1930), 150.

15. For the shortage of iron and for the tools and hardware that were available, see Marc Simmons and Frank Turley, *Southwestern Colonial Ironwork: The Spanish Blacksmithing Tradition from Texas to California* (Santa Fe: Museum of New Mexico Press, 1980), 29, 116–34, 135–61. See, too, Lonn Taylor and Dessa Bokides, *New Mexican Furniture 1600–1940: The Origins, Survival, and Revival of Furniture Making in the Hispanic Southwest* (Santa Fe: Museum of New Mexico Press, 1987).

16. Minge, "Last Will and Testament," 50–52.

17. Albert Pike, *Prose Sketches and Poems Written in the Western Country*, David J. Weber, ed. (Albuquerque: Calvin Horn, 1967), 103.

18. Ibid., 102–03.

19. Ramón A. Gutiérrez, *When Jesus Came, the Corn Mothers Went Away: Marriage, Sexuality, and Power in New Mexico, 1500–1846* (Stanford: Stanford University Press, 1991), 231, describes the practice of giving a newly married son "a cer-

tain number of *vigas* ([roof] "beams"—a way of dividing the space in a house) in the parental home."

20. Minge, "Last Will and Testament," 50. See, too, n. 2 above.

21. By then, the oldest daughter, María Estefana, lived in San Miguel del Vado, married to José Ignacio Lucero, according to family tradition. Fred G. Martínez, *The Story of Antonio Severino Martínez y Lucero de Godoy and María del Carmel Santistevan* (Taos: Kit Carson Memorial Foundation Publications in History, no. 6, 1977), 6.

22. Minge, "Last Will and Testament," 52.

23. Martínez, *The Story of Antonio Severino Martínez*, 12–13, names all eight children. Pascual and Teodora Martínez were the great-grandparents of Fred Martínez.

24. Bunting, *Taos Adobes*, 24, who apparently based this on family tradition.

25. Will of Pascual Martínez, April 4, 1882, Probate Records of Taos County, New Mexico, vol. B–6, p. 281, transcript in Northern New Mexico Abstract and Title Company, Taos, New Mexico, Abstract of Title, no. A–597, copy in KCHM. In 1910, one of the sons of Pascual, also named Severino, sold the house to his brother Agapito, who owned the property immediately to the west. Severino Martínez and his wife, Guadalupe, to Agapito Martínez, February 24, 1910. "*Documento Garantizado*," registered in the County of Taos, 5 October 1931 by J. A. DesGeorges, *Escribano de la Corte de Pruebas y ex-oficio Registrador*. Copy in Northern New Mexico Abstract and Title Company, Taos, New Mexico, Abstract of Title, no. A–597. Xerox copy in KCHM.

26. Bunting, *Taos Adobes*, 23.

27. Letter from Jack K. Boyer to Myra Ellen Jenkins, Taos, December 19, 1973, who obtained this information from the abstract on the property. National Register of Historic Places, nomination form, entry number NR 4–23–73, prepared by James Purdy, archivist, in SRCA, November 2, 1972. This information appears on a final page, consisting of corrections and called "changes." Copy in the Collection of the Cultural Properties Review Committee in SRCA. One Anthony J. Lucero, a Martínez descendant who lived in the house as a child, claimed the sale price was actually $5,000. Lucero to David W. King, State Planning Officer, Washington, D.C., December 5, 1973. Xerox copies in KCHM.

28. Ruth G. Fish, "La Hacienda de Don Pascual Is Located on Río de Pueblo Near Taos," *The Taos Review* (June 1, 1940).

29. Family tradition is reported by Bunting, *Taos Adobes*, 25. However, Fares E. Martínez paid taxes on the property from 1954 to 1964. Certificate of Taxes (1954–1964), prepared by Northern New Mexico Abstract and Title Company, Taos, New Mexico, Abstract of Title, no. A–597. Xerox copy in KCHM. Warranty Deed, January 28, 1964. Copy in Northern New Mexico Abstract and Title Company, Taos, New Mexico, Abstract of Title, no. A–597. Xerox copy in KCHM. For the relationship of Fares Martínez to the family, see Martínez, *The Story of Antonio Severino Martínez*, dedication page and pp. 13–14.

30. Bunting, *Taos Adobes*, 25.

31. Archaeologist John Young, quoted in *Noticias Alegres de la Casa Kit Carson* 9 (October 1977):1–2.

32. Warranty Deed, January 28, 1964. Copy in Northern New Mexico Abstract and Title Company, Taos, New Mexico, Abstract of Title, no. A–597. Xerox copy in KCHM.

33. Undated and unattributed newspaper article, circa 1964 or 1965: "Old Martinez House Under Reconstruction" in KCHM.

34. Divorce decree, filed in Taos County District Court, May 14, 1969 (no. 8225; book W, p. 731), and Certificate of Taxes (1968–1971) prepared by Northern New Mexico Abstract and Title Company, Taos, New Mexico. Copies in Abstract of Title, no. A–597-S–2. Xerox copy in KCHM.

35. "Completion Report on Phase 1—Martínez Project, 1974–78," p. 6, copy in the files of the KCHM. See, too, the notice to the "Descendants of Don Antonio Severino Martínez," February 19, 197[2?], from Jacob Bernal, Chairman, Board of Trustees, Kit Carson Memorial Foundation, and Phil Lovato, Chairman, Spanish Culture Advisory Committee. Copy in KCHM.

36. On September 25, 1970, the Cultural Properties Review Committee of the New Mexico State Planning Office included the house on the State Register of Cultural Properties, a designation

accepted by its owner, Anne Milord. Keith Dotson, State Planning Officer, to Mrs. Annie [sic] Milord, January 22, 1971; Anne Milord to Mr. Dotson, New York, April 29, 1971. In a meeting of September 29, 1972, the Cultural Properties Review Committee of the New Mexico State Planning Office recommended unanimously to nominate the house for the register. Albert Schroeder, chairman, Cultural Properties Review Committee, to Dr. William J. Murtagh, Keeper of the National Register, December 4, 1972. David W. King, State Planning Officer and State Historic Preservation Officer, to Jack K. Boyer, May 16, 1973, informs him of approval. Copy in KCHM.

37. Letter from Phil Lovato to "Descendants of Severino Martínez," Taos, February 21, 1973; and "Martínezes Gather for 'Historic Occasion,'" *Taos News*, April 14, 1973, in KCHM.

38. "Completion Report on Phase 1—Martínez Project, 1974–78," p. 1, in KCHM.

39. Ibid. and other annual reports in the files of the KCHM. For the termination of the CETA program and use of crews through the end, see Jack K. Boyer to Thomas Merlan, Taos, February 6, 1982. An archaeological report for 1975 is unsigned in KCHM.

40. It seems an exaggeration to say that it is "the least altered building of its period that is still habitable," as does Bartholomew, "The Hacienda," 197.

41. Janice Daigh, "Martinez Family Returns to Roots," *Taos News*, October 13, 1983; and Leah Leach, "Martinez Family Meets for Taos Hacienda Dedication," *Albuquerque Journal*, October 8, 1983. Copy in KCHM.

42. Judy Romero, "Old Martinez Mill to Run Again in Live Museum," *Taos News*, January 16, 1986. Copy in KCHM.

43. In his will, don Severino did not specify the location of his mill, but it seems likely that it stood at the same point where his son, Pascual, had a wooden millhouse "with water rights pertaining to said mill" in front of his house, "on the south side" "twenty-five or thirty yards from the house." Will of Pascual Martínez, April 4, 1882, Probate Records of Taos County, New Mexico, vol. B–6, p. 281.

44. For example, Paul Goldberger, "Restoration," *New York Times Magazine* (October 7, 1984): 124–25.

45. For example, Sherry S. Stokes, "Southwestern Holiday Feast," *Cooking Light* (November-December 1993):96–100; James Dao, "What's Doing in Taos," *New York Times* (December 26, 1993); and Alexander O. Boulton, "The Padre's House," *American Heritage* (February–March 1994):93–99.

46. R. C. Gordon-McCutchan to David J. Weber, July 9, 1993, offers these figures: 1989, 23,373; 1990, 27,976; 1991, 33,804; and 1992, 29,271.

47. Quoted in Burl Noggle, "Anglo Observers of the Southwest Borderlands, 1825–1890: The Rise of a Concept," *Arizona and the West* 1 (Summer 1959):129.

Appendix

"The Last Will and Testament
of Don Severino Martínez [1827]"

Edited and Translated by
Ward Alan Minge
Introduction by David J. Weber

In the late 1950s, Ward Alan Minge acquired the original will of Severino Martínez from Tony García of Albuquerque, who had himself obtained it from José Manuel Martínez, the great-grandson of don Severino. Recognizing its unusual completeness and its value for understanding New Mexico material culture at the beginning of New Mexico's Mexican era, Minge painstakingly transcribed and translated the difficult document. Where dictionaries failed, Minge asked old-timers for meanings of words that seemed unique to New Mexico, and he subjected his work to the scrutiny of the late E. Boyd, curator of Spanish Colonial art of the Museum of New Mexico and the leading expert on New Mexico material culture.

The result of Minge's work appeared in the spring of 1963 in the pages of the *New Mexico Quarterly*. With Minge's gracious permission, we here reproduce his article in facsimile. Because the article has been cited frequently, we have retained the pagination from volume 33 of the *New Mexico Quarterly* (the original pagination is noted in square brackets). Through the generosity of Ward Alan Minge, the original will is now in the New Mexico State Records Center and Archives in Santa Fe. Those who wish to consult it will find it there in the Minge Papers—Martínez Collection.

Errata

Dr. Minge offers the following corrections and clarifications to his translation of the will:

p. 36, 7 lines up from bottom: "up to the road" should read "up to the middle road."

p. 38, 11 lines down: Severino's reference to "San Fernando" is to the Río San Fernando.

p. 38, 12 lines down: "the road" should read "the middle road."

p. 38, 14 lines down: "the road" should read "the middle road."

p. 44, 20 lines down: in referring to skins or hides "of mark," here and elsewhere, the executors meant to say of excellent quality ("*de marca*"). Skins or hides described as "of half mark" ("*de media marca*") were "of medium quality."

p. 46, 17 lines down: the typesetter dropped a paragraph, which should follow line 17:

To the son who follows, Don Santiago Martinez, is given 100 pesos in reales, an additional 10 ½ varas of linen, a piece of material "*corte de armador*" at a peso, which because of its poor quality was added the half vara of linen, 10 varas of blanket "*manta*," 5 pounds of sugar, a small pair of scissors, an iron wedge "*calsa de acero*," a pound of iron, 3 pairs of stockings, one serape, 5 hides of mark, 5 hides for camping "camperos," half of a hide, and a deer hide of mark, which in all amounts to 43 pesos 6 reales, 2 horses, two untamed mules, 2 mares, and an ass, all amounting to 245 [pesos] 2 reales.

p. 46, 18 lines down: "Manuel Pascual Martinez" should read Juan Pascual Martinez.

p. 46, 2 lines up: the number of sheep distributed that day were 1,152, together with 60 goats, for a total of 1,212.

Ward Alan Minge
THE LAST WILL AND TESTAMENT OF DON SEVERINO MARTINEZ

Don Severino Martinez was buried at the Church of Our Lady of Guadalupe in Taos, on June 29, 1827. While quite young and in modest circumstances he had married Maria del Carmel Santistevan. Then he owned thirteen cattle, one horse with its saddle in fair condition, and one hundred and seventy-five varas of land. In 1804, the family moved from Abiquiu to Taos and through industriousness and frugality the estate increased manifold. Don Severino, who could read and write, became a leading citizen, holding the important office of alcalde at Taos in 1825. A few weeks before he died, he drew up a will, naming the oldest son, the Priest Don Antonio Jose Martinez, and a son-in-law, Manuel Martinez, as executors. His rather impressive holdings and personal property were passed on to his wife, six children, and two servants.

By this time, the family had become a powerful faction around Taos and the four sons and two sons-in-law took an active part in local politics, the details of which remain fairly obscure. Each increased his respective estate, adding to his inheritance, while gaining considerable regional position, especially Santiago, who served as president of the Departmental Assembly of New Mexico in 1844. Padre Martinez, as verified by the will below, had received some training for the clergy in Durango, Mexico, and later became the spiritual leader for the Rio Arriba area. Today he remains one of the controversial figures of nineteenth-century New Mexico.

His pervasive activities may explain, in part, the hatred that Charles Bent came to demonstrate against the Padre and his family. Bent, trader and future United States governor of the territory, left a lengthly record of this animosity to the United States consul in Santa Fe. His letters scornfully referred to the popular Padre as Mr. Priest, the Great Literary, or the Calf, an epithet often used for Martinez by his enemies. On Christmas day 1842, he wrote, "We have had a dull Christmas here, I believe the Priest was the only merry person in town today, he was quite loving in Beaubien's store today, to great big he-Canadian who nothing would do but he must kiss, and a great many more such tricks, I think he is more sincerely devoted to Baccus than any of the other gods."

The full story of Bent's stubborn opposition to the Martinez clan may never be fully known, although it is certain the Padre reciprocated in kind and was the most outspoken. "The Priest will spare me no means to injure me," Bent wrote on one occasion. Doubtless he was jealous of the Martinez holdings as well as their status in the community, where they were a hindrance to his many ambitions. They meddled in his legal affairs and business enterprises. In exasperation, he wrote the consul that the law was a recourse for "cowards and wimen."

Equally revealing is Bent's contempt for the Padre's "literary career" which had been financed by Don Severino. With sarcasm he wrote in 1841: "As the Priest has resided in one of the most remote sections of the province entirely dependent on his own resources for such an immense knowledge as he has acquired it is astonishing to think how a man could possibly make himself so emminent, in almost every branch of knowledge, that can only be acquired by other men of ordinary capacities, in the most enlightened parts of the world, but as he has extraordinary abilities, he has been able to make himself master of all this knowledge by studying nature in her nudest guise, he is a prodigy, and his great name deserves to be written in letters of gold in all high places that this gaping and ignorant multitude might fall down and worship it, that he has and did condescend to remain amongst us and instruct such a people, it is certainly a great blessing to have such a man amongst us, these people cannot help but find favor in this world and the other world in consequence of having such a man lead and direct them."

The family endured these invectives unscathed and survived Bent, who was murdered in Taos in January 1847. Like many others, they gained a livelihood and strength mainly from productos del pais, produce of the country. The surplus was traded in various parts of Mexico and included many of the items described in the will below: woven blankets and carpeting, buffalo hides, deer skins, beaver, serapes, rebozos, and colchas.

That they guarded these holdings as best they might and through methods which were traditional is shown by the loan to the commissariat for soldiers. Also, they had a torreon at Abiquiu. Nearby, the Suaso family, one of whom witnessed the will, had two such protective structures on their properties around Embudo, where the ruins of one can still be found. In times of stress, the governors considered the area encompassed by El Rito, Abiquiu, Embudo, and Ojo Caliente, one of the defensive frontiers, and expected settlers there to hold their lands against the Indians. Hence, the privately-owned, stone towers, sometimes built with a superstructure of timbers and planking.

The terms of the will are for the most part self-explanatory, but wherever English does not offer an equivalent, the original Spanish word is also indicated. The peso was the Mexican counterpart of the American dollar and consisted of eight reales, at 12½ cents each. It is significant to the economy of this isolated territory to find iron and sugar both worth six reales the pound, while doors, windows, locks, and even portales, or porches, were assigned monetary value. Whiskey sold for around 75 cents the pint. While the family prized products peculiar to the region and possessed few foreign goods, santos or religious objects were not listed. For a comparison, in this same year, a Cristo of wood was appraised at one peso, retablos at two reales each, and retablos in tin frames brought around four pesos.

Also of interest are the detailed instructions for dividing the land among the heirs by partitioning the portions into strips so that each would have access to irrigation or roads. These sections of land were measured off in varas as were the areas encompassed by dwellings and the lengths of cloth and rugs of all kinds. In New Mexico, the vara measured 33.33 inches but was employed somewhat casually in this settlement. At some instances, only the frontage of the field or house seems to be indicated, although square varas appear nearly always to be applied to the latter. Since the vara was equal to a pace, they undoubtedly relied on measurements which had been paced off—yet, measuring sticks were available.

Don Severino's last will is unusual both for its detail and for the careful accounting of its settlement. None of the few known wills of the time are accompanied with a comparable itemized listing with appraisals or such a thorough explanation of final property disposal. The various proceedings for settlement took place from June 30, 1827, through February 20, 1829. In order to keep an accurate recording of the assets and distribution, these were shown in the margins: a running account of the assets was placed on the left margins with distribution shown on the right.

The conscientious manner with which the estate was handled reveals much of interest concerning cultural and economic conditions in New Mexico some one hundred thirty years ago.

The will and settlement were aproved by the Bishop of Durango, Jose Antonio Laureano de Zubiria y Escalante, while on a busy trip into New Mexico in 1833. The citizens had often complained that many years had gone by without the appearance of a bishop, and this visitation ended seventy-three years of such neglect.

The document consists of thirteen numbered pages inscribed with a quill on both sides. The first two numbered pages comprise the will and the remaining eleven, the settlement. The last side carries the approval and signature of the Bishop of Durango. The pages, some large folded and others single, measure approximately 8 inches by 12½ inches and are sewed together on the left-hand side. There are no watermarks or seals.

IN THE NAME OF THE HOLY TRINITY, Father, Son, and Holy Ghost, three distinct persons, and one true God, I, Antonio Severino Martinez, citizen resident of San Geronimo de Taos, in the Territory of New Mexico, being sick, but with my natural judgment, believing as I truly believe, in all the Articles and Mysteries of our Holy Catholic Faith, in which belief I wish and protest to live, and die, as a faithful Christian, and true Catholic, and I hope the Divine Majesty will have mercy for my faults and sins, through the merits of our Lord Jesus Christ, and of his most Holy Mother, whom I elect as advocate in the peril in which I find myself, and so that with my guardian Angel, Saint of my name, and the other Saints of my devotion, will help me in the dreadful Tribunal of God: I make, order, and establish this my testament, and last will, in the following form:

Firstly, I order that my body be buried at the Church of Our Lady of Guadalupe and that the funeral be solemn.

Item, I order that thirty low masses be paid for the benefit of my soul.
Item, I order that the value of twenty pesos be given as alms to the needy poor.

Item, I order that a tract of land, which I will describe below, consisting of ninety varas from the Rio de San Fernando up to the road be divided in equal parts between Maria Gertrudis and Maria Dolores, both now married and who were my servants.

Item, I declare to be indebted on two accounts which have amounted particularly to thirty-six pesos and two reales in goods to my son, the Priest Don Antonio Jose Martinez, and at the rate of cash: I order that the same be paid in the order prescribed in a paper on the matter.

Item, I declare that my said son, the Priest, is indebted to me for six hundred pesos in money, for expenses and costs in his literary career, I order that the same be deducted from his inheritance, or in case the others are paid, and although in said career as specified there were expended of my estate eight hundred and ninety-one pesos, and besides this amount the funeral of his deceased wife, when he became a widower; but I only charge him the said six hundred, for the reason that this is the will of my wife, my children, and mine, and besides all this he has paid for it by not having abandoned me at the time of his marriage and four years that he was a widower before going to his studies, leaving to the total of my estate, the fruit of his work, some small animals which he had, and thirty varas of land which were acknowledged as his, and other loans during the four years he was here after finishing his career of letters.

Item, I declare not to owe anything else and in case any creditor appears attention be paid to the person and proof of what I owe, all of which I leave to the knowledge and discretion of my executors, whose case will be reasonable if any appear.

Item, I declare, that I was married, and kept the first vows with Maria del Carmel Santistevan, at the village of Santo Tomas de Abiquiu, from where I was born, and where we first lived, and then we made our home at this of Taos in the year 1804, from which matrimony we had six children all of whom are living at the present time, and their names in the order of the oldest to the youngest Antonio Jose, Maria Estefana, Juana Maria, Jose Maria de Jesus, Jose Santiago, and Juan Pascual Bailon, youngest of all.

Item, I declare that when I contracted said matrimony I had thirteen head of cattle, one horse with its respective saddle, and in fair condition, one hundred and seventy-five varas of land at the place of my deceased parents, and plaza of the Chapel at Abiquiu which with little change than more or less expense in the partition which I do not have in my possession, but which is in the possession of my nephew, Jose Manuel Salazar, of Abiquiu, and besides this a third part in one hundred varas of land which together with my other two brothers already deceased we designated below the said plaza of the Chapel, and also in equal proportion in a two-room house and a fortification "torrion" at the site of my said deceased parents.

Item, I declare that twenty varas of land, which my said wife obtained as her only inheritance from her parents, were sold said varas of land for a bull, all of which will be taken into consideration, so that after deduction, they will be entered into the assets at my insistence, of my said wife.

Item, I declare to have at the Plaza of the Chapel of Santa Rosa at Abiquiu, besides the referred, one house, deducting the rooms which I traded for another here at Taos to Señora Juana Trujillo, which contains three rooms remaining to me.

Item, I declare to have at the Rito Colorado of Abiquiu one hundred and ten varas of land which are specified in their deed, and one room in the upper Plaza of the said Rito.

Item, I declare to have here in Taos and district of San Francisco del Ranchito in the public plaza, as my own property, and the side of the Rio del Pueblo towards the Rio del Norte, in all about twenty-nine rooms.

Item, one mill in operation in only one room.

Item, in the district of San Fernando, one house started in which five rooms are finished.

Item, I declare to have on the upper part at the said district of San Francisco a tract of land which contains in its deed ninety varas in width and in length from the rio del pueblo to the other side of San Fernando up to the road.

Item, by the same route joining my house one hundred varas of land in width and, in length from the rio del pueblo up to the same road.

Item, one hundred varas of land in width below the Plaza and in length from in front of the same up to the rio del Pueblo, as is described in its document.

Item, from the boundaries of my house in all directions up to the rio del pueblo the land that belonged to Casilda Agilar [sic] to which continuously these last three tracts are adjoining.

Item, from the rio del Pueblo in the direction of the rio del norte as far as the right may be I have four hundred and nine varas of land in width which are contained in four deeds.

Item, in the arroyo hondo and plaza below, one hundred varas of land in width and in length from the river to the ridge as is described by its deed and these are in the lower part.

Item, at the said Plaza of the arroyo hondo one middle-sized room in the house of my niece Trinidad Salazar.

Item, I acknowledge to have for horses with a very small difference of a little less or somewhat more, both old and young, together with the stallion, thirty-six.

Item, twenty-six gentle horses.

Item, twenty-eight mules.

Item, nine burros together with the young.

Item, sixty head of cattle, both young and old and of both gender.

Item, forty-one oxen.

Item, sheep, including both young and old, and both gender, one thousand.

Item, goats, both young and old and both gender, one hundred and a few more.

Item, six hogs with two young.

Item, of merchandise, one hundred sixty varas of linen, ten pairs of scissors, some pieces of material "cortes de armador," eight narrow pieces of blanket "manta," a little whiskey "aguardiente,"* and a little more wine kept each one in its barrel.

Item, one hundred and twenty-four buffalo hides, twenty-five deer hides, forty-four pairs of woolen stockings, and other furniture.

Item, in ready cash or stamped silver, eight hundred pesos.

Item, I declare Jose Maria Meras owes me one hundred pesos cash, I order that the same be collected, security for the payment of which are in my possession articles equalling this debt, which should be returned to him when the hundred pesos are paid.

Item, I declare that the substitute administrator Don Agustin Duran* owes me forty pesos in cash on account of a loan for the soldiers as is recorded in receipts: I order that these be collected.

Item, I declare that there is owing me besides the said, about seven hundred pesos, or somewhat more, which appear in my account book and in other documents of obligations of the debtors: I order that these be collected.

Item, I declare to have four plates, four spoons with their respective forks and a middle-sized cup, all of silver.

Item, I declare to have all the household furnishings, without taking time to enumerate what they may be, in addition to corn, wheat, and vegetables, and also, saddles and trappings for the mules; separating the same from those of my children.

Item, I order that after separating the appropriate portions of my wife and mine, the balance be divided in two parts, one part recognized as assets belonging to my wife, and the other also as assets with my property, be what is recognized as my estate which will be fulfilled as remains ordered, and generally be of the common mass; and the rest be divided among my six children in equal parts, sharing equally the work and cost of collecting what is owed.

Item, I declare and appoint as my legitimate heirs my said six children,

---

*Mexican documents in the period use juisque interchangeably with aguardiente, and sometimes Quintoque juisque—Kentucky whiskey. Aguardiente, however, was made of grapes or black sugar cane syrup. While aguardiente of grapes came from around El Paso and points south, a cane syrup liquor was produced in the north, possibly with a few imported stills but mostly crude, handmade presses and stills. Anglos produced aguardiente in the Taos area during the Mexican period but it is difficult to determine which type of machinery they used even though the central government of Mexico tried to tax the machinery itself from time to time. Clandestine production of whiskey was prohibited but authorities in New Mexico made no effort to subdue it.

*Don Agustin Duran served in various official capacities during the Mexican period (1821-46) in which qualified persons were hard to find. In 1827, his title was commissariat and as such he handled matters for quartering the permanent troops. For a time, he appears as substitute administrator for the military commandant which would explain his title in the text.

as is related, and that they all are legitimate through my faithful marriage, intending it include my two daughters who are now married, their consorts, of Maria Estefana, Don Jose Ygnacio Lucero, and of Juana Maria, Don Jose Manuel Martinez, and the other three, all of whom I placed in the estate of matrimony; with the exception of the youngest, Juan Pascual, who consequently will be rewarded proportionately out of the common.

Item, I leave as my testamentary executors, and executors of my will, Don Antonio Jose Martinez, my oldest son, and Don Manuel Martinez, my son-in-law, to whom, and to each of whom, in the entirety "Solidam," I give all my due power, as much right as is required, so that they may be able to enter, and enter upon all my estates and may distribute the same, as best they may judge and agree, and as is directed in this testament, and I give them permission in order that they may be able to substitute in their duties and substitute others in their steads, so that they may carry the same into due execution, whom I immediately recognize as appointed, and give them the same permission and power, of the above named.

Item, I want and it is my will that all placed in my testament up to here be fulfilled by my executors, according to the material and literal order of its clauses.

Item, by this my testament, I revoke, annul, and admit no other testament whatever, or testaments, codicil, or codicils, that I may have made, and granted, so that the same may have no value nor any effect in judgment, nor outside of it, now or at any time, that the same may appear and be shown, even if it have annulling clauses, and particular words, of which special mention may have to be made, of which I do not remember at the present time, and if they should come to mind, I would repeat the same de verbo ad verbum, all of which I desire to have no value; and at the same time I wish to have no value or effect any testament or testaments which I may henceforth make, unless I may make expressed mention of this clause that I hereto place, since resolutely I wish this present disposition be valid in every case as my testament and last will in the form and manner, that best do justice, which testament I grant at the plaza of San Fernando de San Geronimo de Taos on the eighth day of the month of June of 1827.

SEVERINO MARTINEZ

It is recorded by me that this testament was made and granted in San Geronimo de Taos, Plaza of San Fernando, by the grantor, Don Severino Martinez, who, although he is sick, is in his entire and sane judgment, on this eighth day of June 1827, which grantor I know and give faith, and he came before me, Don Manuel Martinez, Constitutional Alcalde of this jurisdiction, in the company of five witnesses who are the citizens Jose Antonio Suaso, Jose Tafoya, Tomas Romero, Manuel Baca, and Pablo Blea,

AT SAN GERONIMO DE TAOS on the thirtieth day of the month of June in the year one thousand eight hundred and twenty-seven the appointed executors, Don Antonio Jose Martinez and Don Jose Manuel Martinez, for our deceased father, Don Severino Martinez, to begin to fulfill the commands and orders in the foregoing testament place this writ, in which we accepted the commission for beginning, we assert that the funeral rites and burial made yesterday as is ordered were exercised with a mass in presence of the body and with other solemnities: the expense, four wax candles the second executor furnished as his part and at his expense, and twenty candles by the first executor, for which they make no charge: to the Priest Don Juan Felipe Ortiz,* who was asked to officiate, the Parish Priest not being able to comply because of the circumstances, was given as compensation the sum of thirty pesos in money, and twenty for the masses which are specified in the testament for which he gave a voucher, which is attached at the beginning, and the other ten for which as many pesos were given, appear also in note, some and others, although it is not explained in the notes, the admonition was made that in this year all the masses have to be said, and furthermore, as soon as possible. To the two chanters to each one three pesos more not in money, and to the sacristan two, all of which will be specified further on: the cost of the coffin has not been ascertained, which will also be explained hereafter, and for the tolling of the bells and for other things, which may accumulate, no charge is made by the Parish Priest, his son, and no charge will be made for other functions which they will attempt to do for the deceased on the seventh day after the burial, and on the thirteenth, and for the due record, we sign this writ.

ANTONIO JOSE MARTINEZ   MANUEL MARTINEZ

AT SAN GERONIMO DE TAOS on the second day of the month of July of one thousand eight hundred and twenty-seven, the executors of the

---

*Later to become Vicar at Santa Fe and strongly anti-Anglo, he was responsible for charging foreigners exhorbitant marriage fees. Governor Manuel Armijo, while despotic in many other facets of his government, allowed the Vicar a free hand in church affairs.

all residents of this jurisdiction, and they were called for said purpose, the same who signed with me and those who could not write placed a cross, of which I attest.

TOMAS ROMERO
JOSE ANTONIO SUASO
MANUEL BACA   +
JOSE TAFOYA
PABLO BLEA

foregoing statement, in fulfilling their commission, proceed with the arrangements which in specifications are the following with appraisement of the goods for better clarification and distribution, namely:

Of the linen contained in the testament, there only exists, in favor of the credit side, ninety-one varas, calculated as fourteen of cotton cloth "pontiví" at 12 reales the vara, and the balance at one peso. Of the pieces of blanket "manta," which are narrow, three pieces of thirty and one-half varas at 3 reales the vara; and the balance of the linen and blanket which are specified in the testament were given to Jose Maria and to Santiago, children of the deceased, for what was due to them of the goods, which were besides the expenses and were well examined and faithfully delivered completing the said account with horses, which afterwards mention will be made at another place.

A cashmere shawl "tapalo de casimir" at five pesos, two small cotton shawls at two each, a handkerchief five reales and two small ones at three reales. Seven varas of calico "indiana" at a peso, four pieces of quilt "colchado" at a peso four reales each one, and one blue rebozo three pesos and four reales. Twelve pounds of iron at 6 reales the pound, 60 pounds sugar at 6 reales, which all amounts to 54 pesos, multiplying and adding. Of the whiskey "aguardiente" which the testament cites nothing exists, because part was used, and the money which was accumulated for the part that was sold will appear in the silver. Of the wine described there were paid to the Priest of the debt twenty-six pints at five reales for each of the accounts in the testament which are sixteen pesos and two reales: for one pound of sugar and one bottle of wine with two more reales, one peso and three reales: for twenty-seven varas of narrow blanket "manta" at the prices of Chihauhua at which price they were purchased by him belongs five pesos four reales: for a blue rebozo two pesos two reales for the same reason, and for two varas of wool six reales, which in all were paid him the two accounts and still owing to him ten.

There remained 16 pints of wine computed at 4 reales each.

To the chanter Ortega there were given as his dues for which he sang three pesos, he owes the balance which is found in the book of accounts. The Priest Don Antonio Martinez paid for the account as explains the clause of his debt, to the other chanter Blea three pesos, to the sacristan two, and to the carpenter for the box 7 pesos, to the same account he paid out in distribution of alms the twenty pesos as specified, and to give evidence of what are given them. He paid twelve buffalo hides of new mark at two pesos, and twelve hides for camping "camperos" of mark at a peso. He paid a quilt "colcha" at six pesos, and a woven, woolen blanket "fresada atilmada" at another six, both of quality. And he paid, finally, three hundred and twenty pesos in cash which in all are four hundred, leaving a balance of two hundred pesos for next year, this payment taking care of the ten pesos of money restored to him. At this place belong the thirty pesos to the curate Don Juan Felipe as a gift, and the other thirty which appear in notes for the masses of the testament.

But, the pesos which the clause orders collected from Jose Maria Meras were paid by him, there were one hundred and two, there were given him two obligations that he had, and there were found returned to him his articles. Also, in cash, the eight hundred which the testament mentions counting in these the sixty for the funeral and masses. For money which was paid in after the will, either for the little whiskey which was sold or for other emoluments there are thirty-nine pesos one-half real: which is with all the stamped money, together with the estimated wrought silver, all that the testament cites, one hundred pesos, 1,361 pesos ½ real, with which is terminated the transaction, and acknowledged this day, which we, the executors, signed for due record.

Antonio Jose Martinez   Manuel Martinez

At San Geronimo de Taos on the seventh day of the month of July one thousand eight hundred and twenty-seven, we the testamentary executors proceed to distribute and to bring to an end that contained in the foregoing declaration and to which is added in this, and is as follows:

There enter into the assets the hides of the will, forty-eight of mark at two pesos, and forty-eight hides for camping "camperos" at a peso, and thirty of half mark at ten reales each, all of which amounts to one hundred and eighty-one pesos and four reales. Twelve half hides at two reales are three pesos. Five deer skins of mark at 20 reales, six of half mark at ten reales, and fourteen small ones of all kinds at 10 pesos, amounting in all to 30 pesos.

Twenty-nine varas of woolen sheeting "sabanilla" at 2 reales are 7 pesos 2 reales. Nine light serapes at 4 reales are 4 pesos 4 reales. Forty pairs of stockings at 4 reales the pair, and other pairs were woolen at a real making 20 pesos 4 reales. There further appeared another narrow piece of blanket "manta" 30 varas at the aforesaid price, excepting therefrom the half which has been counted, are 5 pesos 4 reales. The ten scissors at 3 reales are 3 pesos 6 reales. One saber with the hilt and guard in a scabbard of silver, although worth more, it was appraised by the agreement of all at 25 pesos.

Of the herd: 21 horses at 12 pesos each one are 252. Mules in all 29 at 25 pesos are 725 pesos, twenty-two mares with two colts all at 8 pesos, are 192 pesos, three year-old colts at 4 pesos are 12 pesos, seven of the same born this year at 1 peso 4 reales are a total of 10 pesos 4 reales. Six fullgrown burros at 7 pesos 4 reales are 45 pesos, three young burros at 6 pesos each are 18 pesos.

All the assets up to here set forth in the testament by continuation of its settlement, with the money realized and the effects appraised, are a total of 3,206 pesos 3½ reales, one-half of which belongs to the widow, our mother, 1,603 pesos 1 real and ¾, and the remainder to the heirs, and it was ordered one hundred pesos of wrought silver, and five hundred and eighty pesos in cash be given to our mother, and in goods 7 varas of cotton cloth "pontivi" and 24½ varas of linen, 7 varas of calico "indiana" and 60 varas of blanket "manta," the three shawls "tapalos," the rebozo, the three small handkerchiefs, the 16 pints of wine, 4 scissors, and six iron wedges "calsas de acero" which were not included in the assets at a real each one, which all this amounts to 88 pesos 5 reales. Also, twenty-two pairs of stockings, four pairs woolen socks "escarpines," 14½ varas of woolen sheeting "sabanilla," three small serapes, 30 hides of mark, 15 of half mark, 30 hides for camping "camperos," 6 half hides, two deer hides of mark, and 14 small aforesaid, altogether amounting to 141 pesos 7 reales. Also, nine horses together with the two stallions, 14 mules, the two large colts, ten mares, the three little colts one-year old, and the seven born this year: the three little burros, all of which amounts to 594 pesos 4 reales. Finally, there was given to her 30 pounds of sugar, and all which was given to her amounted to 1,516 pesos 2 reales, transferring to her the six reales of iron, the other six wedges were shared by the heirs, and the balance which hereafter will be paid to her: 6 pounds of iron.

For the formal immutability, the Priest gave from distributed assets the twenty pesos in alms to the needy poor and this order remains concluded.

To the oldest son, the Priest Don Antonio Jose Martinez, was given of that up to here enumerated: 100 pesos in cash, 7 varas of cotton cloth "pontivi," 10 varas of blanket "manta," 5 pounds of sugar, a pair of scissors, one iron wedge "calsa de acero," one pound of iron, all this besides the money amounts to 19 pesos 2 reales. Also, three pairs of stockings, the third part of 14½ varas of sheeting "sabanilla" at 10 reales, 1 serape, 5 hides of mark, two of half mark, 5 hides for camping "camperos," 1 half hide, 2 deer skins of half mark, which amounts to 23 pesos 4 reales. Two horses, two mules, two mares, one burro, all of which amounts to 97 pesos 4 reales.

To the daughter who follows, Maria Estafana, and to her husband, Don Ygnacio Lucero, were delivered: 100 pesos in cash, 10 varas of linen, 10 varas of blanket "manta," 5 pounds of sugar, one pair of scissors, one hoe "cabador," which enters in the assets at two pounds and two ounces at two reales, one iron wedge "calsa de acero," one pound of iron, one piece of material "corte de armador," three pairs of stockings, one serape, five hides of mark, 3 half mark, five hides for camping "camperos," a half hide, two deer skins of half mark, all of which, excepting the cash are 46 pesos. Also, two horses, two mules, two mares, one ass, and this amounts to ninety-seven pesos four reales.

To the next daughter, Juana Maria, were delivered: one hundred pesos in cash, ten varas of linen, ten pounds of blanket "manta," five pounds of sugar, one pair of scissors, one iron wedge "calsa de acero," one pound of iron, one piece of material "corte de armador," three pairs of stockings, one serape, five hides of mark, two of half mark, five hides for camping "camperos," a half hide, one deer skin of mark, and a third part of the fourteen and one-half varas of woolen sheeting "sabanilla," all of which amounts to forty-three pesos and six reales, outside the money before cited.

Also, two horses, two mules, two mares, and one ass, which amounts to 97 pesos 4 reales.

To the son who follows, Don Jose Maria Martinez, were delivered one hundred pesos in cash, ten and one-half varas of linen, one piece of material "corte de armador" at one peso for being of inferior quality he was granted the one-half vara of linen, ten varas of blanket "manta," five pounds of sugar, one pair of scissors, one iron wedge "calsa de acero," one pound of iron, three pairs of stockings, one serape, five hides of mark, three of half mark, five hides for camping "camperos," a half hide, and one deer skin of mark, all of which amounts to forty-three pesos six reales. Two horses, two mules, two mares, and one ass, all amounting to 241 pesos 2 reales.

To the youngest son, Don Manuel Pascual Martinez, were delivered one hundred pesos in cash, and in conformity with the testamentary clause to the effect that no expenses were incurred to marry him, we determine to grant to him as his inheritance from our deceased father fifty pesos in cash, of which twenty pesos were delivered to him, leaving a balance of five and the other twenty-five pesos were given to him in the aforementioned saber, it being the duty of the widow, our mother, to marry him with the help of this, and whatever she pleases, also, eleven and one-half varas of linen, ten varas of blanket "manta," five pounds of sugar, one pair of scissors, one iron wedge "calsa de acero," one pound of iron, three pairs of stockings, one serape, five hides of mark, three of half mark, five hides for camping "camperos," a half hide, and two deer skins of half mark, which are, together with two horses, two mules, two mares, and one ass, in all two hundred and sixty-one pesos and six reales.

There was also given to our widowed mother, the heavy, woven blanket "fresada atilmada" and the quilt "colcha," above mentioned, 12 pesos. What remains without having been distributed, and which was not divided equally according to the inventory, which is being taken together with the distribution, will be disposed of afterwards, and so that it will appear on record we, the executors, sign.

Antonio Jose Martinez Manuel Martinez

[On August 2, 1827, Antonio Jose Martinez and Manuel Martinez distributed the sheep of which 1,552 were counted and appraised at 6 reales each.]

LAST WILL AND TESTAMENT

[On October 1, 1827, Antonio Jose Martinez and Manuel Martinez distributed the cattle of which 98 were counted and appraised at 8 pesos for cows, 10 pesos for bulls, 2 pesos for calves.]

At Taos on the fifteenth of April in the year of one thousand eight hundred and twenty-eight, I, Don Antonio Jose Martinez, for the other executor to this testament, Don Manuel Martinez, having died, substitute in his place my brother, Don Santiago Martinez, conforming to the terms of the testamentary clause, so that he will assist me in the settlement of this will, and we both proceed on this day to set down in writing the matters of partition, placing what there may be of the assets and of the distribution, in the following way:

The succeeding have been delivered to our mother: one iron grate "parrilla de fierro" at four reales, six scythes "oses" at two reales each, three axes at two pesos four reales each, and eleven hoes "cabadores" placed at eight pesos considering they are not complete, they are appraised each one at eighteen reales, two traps for hunting beaver at ten pesos each, four blunderbusses "trabucos" at two pesos apiece, one saw at six reales, one iron spindle and two cranks "malacate con dos siguenas" at four reales, one iron shovel at two pesos, one scale with weights "romana con su cursor" at ten pesos, some balances of yellow metal "balansas de metal amarilla" together with its frame three pesos, two pairs wool cards "cardas" at four pesos, they are old and incomplete, two barrels at six pesos each one, and three more at three pesos each, ninety fanegas of wheat at a peso, and thirty sacks of corn at four reales, one broken wagon twenty-five pesos, fourteen pack saddles with their equipment and ropes at four pesos each, and twelve sacks at one peso, all of which amounts in assets and distribution, 290 pesos 6 reales.

Also, two mules which were not distributed above at the price therein calculated, these were given to our mother, and as already placed in the assets they are only shown in distribution, the value of fifty pesos.

One branding iron at three pesos.

Also, two horses at fourteen pesos: of the land of the Cañada which extends to the north my mother received two hundred and eight varas, and they were given to her those from the wall adjoining the placita one hundred and eighty, and the ninety above from the Rio de San Fernandez to that of the Pueblo, on account of it having been so specified, those lands

---

Overleaf facsimile: Two pages from codicils to the Will of Don Severino Martinez. The value of the assets is listed in the left margins and distribution is shown in the right margins.

which follow from the River to the road running through them, to Gertrudis and to Maria Dolores, one hundred varas, and the vara appraised for all at one peso in cash, the mill together with all its appurtenances at thirty pesos, the house adjoining the mill at the above said land at ten pesos, and one small house which is along the bank of the irrigation ditch on the section above near the ridge, terminated the work, at four pesos, all of this amounts to three hundred and eighty pesos.

Also, at the large house on the plaza of San Francisco del Ranchito there was given to her the room with the plank roof, and the little room with a plank roof, which together with thirteen and one-half varas at a peso and six reales the vara, with two doors, two windows, and one padlock "candado," these at a peso: the little room with a basement and with a small portal and picket fence "varandal" seven varas at one peso the vara, and the door of the basement with also the small portal of the room and four varas of that of the hall "sala" at four reales the vara. The old house on the corner of the plaza containing eleven varas, and the same additional varas in the upper story at twelve pesos because it is falling and needs repairs. The house that belonged to the deceased Garcia, in very bad condition contains twenty-two varas at 4 reales for the same reason: the walled corral, the corral of posts, and another with posts, on the boundary of Luceros, and another at the Arroyo Seco on the small farm with the little house, all this at fifteen pesos. And finally, the house at San Fernandez with five rooms, explained in the testamentary clause, in its enclosure containing forty-three varas at two pesos the vara: all this last amounts, together with the furniture "amaron" of the little store to fifteen pesos, the double door "puerta de dos manos," six single doors, and three windows twelve pesos: are one hundred and eighty-nine pesos five reales, all of which is set down in the assets and go to its settlement.

There were delivered to Maria Dolores, and to Maria Gertrudis, servants, the ninety varas from the Rio de San Fernando to the road forty-five varas to each one, the vara was appraised at four reales. There are also placed here in the distribution, the twenty pesos which were forgotten last year, which were paid out by the first executor, under the terms described above, since then given as alms to the needy poor. It was not forgotten, 20 pesos.

To the oldest brother there was given in this declaration the following: two clocks, and some pieces of iron for the work of hoeing and chopping, two jugs, fifteen fanegas of wheat, five sacks of corn, one pack saddle with its equipment and ropes, and two saddle bags for six pesos, fifty varas of land which formerly belonged to the deceased Felipe Varela, and the walled corral mentioned in the testamentary clause, on the plaza of San Fernandez, now fallen, and because it needs rebuilding, at ten pesos, all of this amounts to, together with a branding iron, and the right which belonged to the children of the deceased Concepcion Romero, at three pesos, to ninety-five pesos and two reales, all of which enter in the assets, and pass to the distribution.

To the sister who follows, Maria Estafana, and as her death has happened, in favor of her children Maria Petra, and the others who are five, with the due relation which has been heretofore made and other formalities, which at the time of the granting will be exacted for them, besides the hoe of last year, one iron link chain (these gifts are in place of the axe), one file, three augers, fifteen fanegas of wheat, five sacks of corn, one saddle with its equipment and ropes, and two saddle bags that since last year were taken by her husband Lucero, father of the said children of the above deceased, and there was charged to him one horse at fourteen pesos, which was sold to him besides another which he had also received, this second horse was donated to all of his children by our deceased father, there was also given to them fifty varas of land of that which is adjoining below those of the oldest brother, and of the same dimensions as found in the deed for the land: there was also assigned to them the house that was Juana Trujillo's, which is at the entrance of the plaza of San Francisco del Ranchito, fifteen and one-half varas below, as many others in the upper story, and two doors with iron locks "chapa de fierro," all of this amounts to forty-nine, and together with the rest one hundred and thirty-nine to the two margins and one or two reales.

To the sister who follows, Juana Maria, there was delivered the following: one hoe, one axe, for which the equivalent was given a meat carver "tranchete"; two scythes, one jug, one pack saddle together with its furnishings and two saddle bags, one horse at fourteen pesos: fifteen fanegas of wheat, and five sacks of corn: fifty-one varas of land at the boundary of the Pueblo and Rio de Lucero to the banks of the Rio del Norte, following the land of our mother: and the house was given her that used to belong to the deceased Felipe Varela, the upper and lower stories containing thirty-one varas in all, with two doors, iron lock, one of those, and a window, all at the estimated price, amounts to: one hundred and forty-five pesos, and six reales.

To the brother who continues, Jose Maria de Jesus, the following: one hoe, and in place of the axe there were given to him some broken bridles, and some small pieces of iron: one musket "fusil" at eight pesos, two scythes, one jug, one pack saddle together with its furnishings, less saddle bags at four pesos, one horse at fourteen pesos, the saddle "silla" of our deceased father, found to be broken, at three pesos, some cushions "coginillos" at two, fifteen fanegas of wheat, five sacks of corn, fifty-one varas of land continuing below that of Juana and for a house the large hall "sala mayor" at the main residence at Ranchito de San Francisco, sixteen varas at a peso and six reales each for having a planked floor, the double doors "puerta de dos manos" at the same house at two pesos, the window at one: the storeroom "dispensa" which continues from the hall in the same line, ten varas, at twelve reales, its door and iron lock two pesos, and the portal belonging to the large hall, which measures nine varas at four reales, besides the four varas of our mother, which altogether amounts to one hundred and fifty-nine pesos and two reales, in assets and distribution.

To our brother following him, Jose Santiago, there was given: one hoe, and axe, one musket "fusil" at eight pesos, one jug, two scythes, one pack saddle equipped excepting the bags, at four pesos, one horse at fourteen pesos, fifteen fanegas of wheat, five sacks of corn, fifty-one varas of land adjoining that of Jose Maria, and for house the storeroom that continues which contains a partition, consisting of fifteen varas at the same twelve reales, its door and iron lock two pesos, and the room which continues from this one up to the passageway "saguan" at the said estimate of nine and one-half varas, also its door and window one peso and four reales, and the portal which corresponds to these appraised at six pesos, all of which amounts to one hundred and forty-eight pesos, to the assets and settlement.

To the youngest brother, Juan Pascual, the following: hoe and axe, one musket "fusil" at eight pesos, one jug and two scythes: one pack saddle with its furnishings without saddle bags, at four pesos, a horse at fourteen pesos, fifteen fanegas of wheat, five sacks of corn, fifty-one varas of land adjoining that of the foregoing, the house which is on the same land, which he received on the boundary of the said Lucero, twenty varas at the said price, two doors, and one window three pesos, and finally, one small room made of boards with its little hall, which adjoins the room of our mother to the passageway "saguan," with its two doors, and two windows and iron lock at sixteen pesos for these all of which amounts to one hundred and fifty pesos and six reales. Also, one mule of those already counted in the inventory, and of which no disposition had been made, at twenty-five pesos. With which is terminated the act of this day, and for the due permanency we, the said executors, sign on the aforesaid date.

Antonio Jose Martinez
Santiago Martinez

In order to equalize that which has been done up to here, of which due notice has to be taken, we, the executors, place the following memorandum, for the purpose that investigating the differences, to proceed further with what there is after observation.

There has been given to our mother conforming to what has been covered in the entire proceeding .... 3,229. 3.
To the bequests of the same terms .... 140. 0.
To the oldest brother .... 479. 2.

LAST WILL AND TESTAMENT

To Maria Estefana	526. 4.
To Juana Maria	530. 6.
To Jose Maria de Jesus	544. 2.
To Jose Santiago	533. 0.
To Juan Pascual	613. 0.
	3,366. 6.

One peso that was deducted on two pieces of material for its inferior quality, another peso was left over after the division and does not appear in the assets, and a half real, all of which are here placed

$$2.\ 1/2$$
$$3,368.\ 6\,1/2$$

and some errors, which were incurred during the proceedings, now are corrected in their proper places, and seven reales less, which have to be deducted from the assets on account of having been in excess.

To equalize the respective distribution to our mother, it is hereby agreed that there be given to her; deducting the twelve head of cattle, which in one will balance, and the horse with the entire saddle and furnishings one hundred and ten pesos, which are left in favor of the heirs, and bequests. There was given to our mother two large, used carpets *"alfombras"* at five pesos, four mattresses *"colchones"* at five pesos each, six linen sheets at three pesos each, four pillows *"almoadas"* at four pesos, one heavy, woven blanket at four pesos, and three of the same without designs at two pesos, this was besides that which was bequeathed to her for that issued by right, two day beds *"camapeses"* at three pesos, four stools *"taburetes"* at four reales, two large tables at four pesos, one cabinet *"almario"* at three pesos, two large boxes for clothes *"cajones de roperos"* with their iron locks at five pesos each, one grain box *"cajon arinero"* two pesos, four carts with their respective equipment at eight pesos each, fence posts at seven pesos, the construction of the tumbled wall near the house seven pesos, and repaired by this account, forty varas of woolen rug *"gerga"* at two reales, one deer skin, woolen sheeting *"sabanilla"*, serapes, stockings, and other emoluments which were delivered to her last year without having been accounted for, of which was paid into common assets, the amount of thirty-nine pesos and two reales, all of which totals one hundred and seventy-six pesos and two reales, to the assets, and settlement. There enter into the assets one hundred and sixteen pesos and two reales, paid by the Priest out of the two hundred pesos remaining for this purpose since last year. Also the forty pesos owed by Don Agustin Duran, and twenty-three pesos six reales which have been paid in cash by the debtors, all of which amounts to one hundred and eighty pesos for the assets, out of these were given to our mother as the amount belonging to her, ninety pesos.

To the oldest son, the Priest, were given the eighty-three pesos and two reales left over from the said two hundred pesos, and as ready cash enter the assets and settlement. There were also given to him nine pesos in cash, and one large, gilded mirror *"espejo grande dorado"* appraised at six.

To the sister Maria Estefana, and for her children, being now deceased, in guardianship of the oldest brother, hides for camping *"camperos,"* four at a peso, four buffalo hides of mark at two pesos each, four pairs of stockings at four reales, a serape with designs in color *"atilmado de piañas"* at four pesos, a woolen rug *"gerga"* of five varas at a peso, a large woolen rug *"gergon"* of eleven varas two pesos six reales, thirty varas of woolen sheeting *"sabanilla"* at two reales the vara, one box at three pesos, eight varas of woolen rug *"gerga"* at two pesos, and in silver seventeen pesos and two reales, are for settlement in cash, not in assets, excepting only the property, fifty-one pesos four reales.

To Juana Maria two buffalo hides of mark at two pesos, another of the same of half mark a peso four reales, a *"conchege"* at two reales, one pair of stockings at four reales, two serapes with designs five pesos for both, 11 varas of woolen rug *"gergon"* two pesos six reales, two woolen rugs *"gergas"* of five varas each two pesos, nine ordinary serapes four pesos four reales, nineteen varas of woolen sheeting *"sabanilla"* at four pesos six reales, one linen sheet three pesos, that amounts to thirty pesos two reales to both margins and seventeen pesos in silver.

To Jose Maria, two buffalo hides of mark at two pesos, one pair of stockings at four reales, a serape with designs at three pesos, a woven blanket at two pesos, a medium-sized serape at one peso, six ordinary serapes at four reales each, one belt *"faja"* six reales, one box three pesos, one bunch of tobacco four reales, and a silver peso, they are eighteen pesos six reales, also in cash noted sixteen pesos.

To Jose Santiago two buffalo hides of mark at two pesos each, a hide for camping *"campero"* a peso, one pair of tooled-leather boots at three pesos, one bunch of tobacco at four reales, one box at three pesos, one large woolen rug *"gergon"* eleven varas, two pesos six reales, one woolen rug *"gerga"* a peso, one pair of stockings four reales, one blanket with designs four pesos, one serape with designs in color three pesos, nine ordinary serapes four pesos four reales, seven varas of woolen sheeting *"sabanilla"* peso and six reales, which amounts to twenty-nine pesos, and in silver sixteen pesos.

And lastly, to the youngest son, Juan Pascual, fifteen pesos. With which was terminated this act which in order that it will appear of record, and having made the division, all equal in his legitimate share, and our mother with her half, we, the executors sign the declaration.

Antonio Jose Martinez
Santiago Martinez

At San Geronimo de Taos on the twentieth day of the month of February of the year 1829, the testamentary executors, for the purpose of terminating settlement of the will, proceed to verify precisely what there is of the collection, and other effects that belong in the common assets.

With the consent and agreement of the children, heirs, there is left in favor of our widowed mother, Maria del Carmel Santistevan, that which has not been paid, either in obligations, or outstanding notes which there are in the book of accounts, although many of these last debts have been denied, many by those who created them availing themselves of the pretext of having no obligation in writing, and what may be paid of the remaining debts according to the referenced, of what remains be paid, and is received in goods by our mother.

One black Turkish cloth was given for thirty masses, their aplication to be in favor of our deceased father, appears in a voucher given and signed for whom they applied. The balance of the clothing of our deceased father was disposed by agreement and is not set down here.

On these last proceedings there was given to our mother the following at its appraisal: two hides of mark at 2 pesos, one buffalo hide half mark twelve reales, one braided rope four reales, two pounds of beaver five pesos, one serape of many colors and designs, and two woolen blankets of colors and designs at 6 pesos each, six pints of whiskey from El Paso at six reales, the six hogs mentioned in the testamentary clause at 8 pesos each, the house and land at Arroyo Hondo, which appears in their deed at forty pesos, the house containing four rooms which is situated at Abiquiu, Plaza de la Capilla, at thirty-eight pesos, three bunches of tobacco at two reales, fifty-five varas of woolen sheeting "*sabanilla*" at two reales, which all amounts to one hundred and thirty-eight pesos. Also, the tract of land at the place of La Talaya, and that of the Rio de San Cristoval.

The third part of the land at Abiquiu with the Salazars was given to the same for three masses for our deceased father which will be added to a voucher. And in regard to the house and fortified place "*torrion*" which belong to the assets of our deceased father, we agree that if there is someone who may purchase them, the proceeds be applied to masses for the souls in Purgatory.

To the oldest son, one of the executors, there were given fifteen fanegas of wheat at the Rito Colorado, and the land containing one hundred and ten varas, and the house at the same Rito was given to the son, giving seventy-two pesos in cash, of which they owed him for his legitimate share in this declaration, eight pesos. And of the land of our deceased father at Abiquiu, they gave him his share in twenty-nine varas at the upper part at sum of 2 reales the vara, they are seven pesos two reales.

To the children of the deceased Estefana there were given in this declaration, one hide for camping, and a pair of stockings for twelve reales, and in silver twenty-one pesos and four reales, and 29 1/6 varas of land at Abiquiu adjoining those of the oldest brother.

To the sister who follows, Juana Maria, twelve reales, and in silver 21 pesos 4 reales, one blanket "*tilma*," and the land which adjoins that of Estefana, 29 1/6 varas at the said appraisement.

To the brother who follows, Jose Maria, was given one mule at 22 pesos and a peso in silver, and land adjoining that of Juana at Abiquiu, 29 1/6 varas.

To the brother who follows, Jose Santiago, twelve pesos four and one-half reales, and what is lacking to him of his 23, a mule which is lost, and at all risks, and the said land at Abiquiu the 29 varas, and the sixth, adjoining that of Jose Maria.

To the youngest, Juan Pascual, one mule and a peso, for the 23, and the twenty-nine varas and sixth of the land already mentioned at Abiquiu, and the lower part at the same value.

Here there were added the thirty pesos of the Turkish cloth for as many more masses to the two margins. And there were in conclusion, as well evidenced, the seven thousand five hundred and seven pesos, two and one-half reales, distributed in the common assets, delivered the corresponding considerations, and executed the bequests and contents of the testament, what is contained, passed adequately, in both margins, leaving unfinished only that which will be placed in a succeeding declaration whenever the father of the children of the deceased Estefana returns. And it will be necessary to enjoin, all the parties will sign, for the record, and as a receipt of what was delivered to them, and so that it will appear of record, we, the executors sign this declaration, today above cited.

Antonio Jose Martinez
Santiago Martinez
Ygnacio Lucero
Juana Maria Martinez
Jose Maria Martinez

San Fernando de Taos, July [day destroyed in the original], 1833
I visited this will in all piety and approved it

The Bishop of Durango

Acknowledgments

Many people gave generously of their time to answer questions and share information with me: Jan Barnhart of the Center for Southwest Research at the University of New Mexico; Malcolm Ebright of Guadalupita, New Mexico; Sandra Jaramillo and Richard Salazar of the State Records Center and Archives in Santa Fe; Jennifer Keen of Dallas, Texas; John Kessell, professor of history at the University of New Mexico; Tony Mares, professor in the English Department at North Texas University; Rowena Martínez of Taos, owner of the Pascual Martínez Papers; Vicente M. Martínez, acting chief curator at the Millicent Rogers Museum in Taos; Father Juan Romero of San Francisco Church in Los Angeles; Marc Simmons of Cerrillos, New Mexico; and Professor Tom Steele, S.J., of Regis College in Denver.

Several people not only answered questions along the way but also read the entire manuscript, pointing out errors and infelicities. For those time-consuming readings I am indebted to my good friend Janet Lecompte of Moscow, Idaho, who has improved my work on New Mexico for three decades; Corina Aurora Santistevan, archivist for the Church of San Francisco de Asis in Ranchos de Taos, whose knowledge of local history is peerless; the eagle-eyed John O. Baxter of Santa Fe, who has mastered the documentary sources; David and Carol Farmer of Dallas, friends and fellow *aficionados* of the Southwest and its literature; and my in-house editor and counselor-at-law, Carol Bryant Weber.

My one-time *compañero de clase* and occasional mentor, Ward Alan Minge of the Casa San Ysidro in Corrales, New Mexico, played two roles in the making of this book. First, he critiqued the manuscript and provided guidance along the way. Second, he acquired Severino Martínez's will, translated it, published it, and donated the original to a public repository. In so doing, he made it possible to tell Severino Martínez's story more fully and to restore his house with greater fidelity.

At the Kit Carson Historic Museums in Taos, I am grateful to R. C. Gordon-McCutchan, who persuaded me to do this project in the first place and who then responded to my frequent requests for information. Skip Miller, codirector and curator, gave me his personal attention in Taos and, with his wife and my friend, art historian Liz Cunningham, wonderful hospitality.

At my own university, Southern Methodist, which maintains a summer campus at Fort Burgwin high above the Taos Valley (founded in 1852 and named for Capt. John H. K. Burgwin, who died during the Taos Rebellion of 1847), I am grateful for support from the Robert and Nancy Dedman Chair in History, to the peerless William B. Taylor, and to my able research assistant Jane Elder, who has made this and other books happen.

Abbreviations Used in the Notes

AASF = Archives of the Archdiocese of Santa Fe (references are to the roll and frame number of the microfilm edition).

KCHM = Kit Carson Historic Museums.

MANM = Mexican Archives of New Mexico (references are to the roll and frame number of the microfilm edition).

NMHR = *New Mexico Historical Review.*

PMP = Pascual Martínez Papers. Xerox copies are on file at the Millicent Rogers Museum, Taos, New Mexico. I consulted these with the gracious permission of their owner, Rowena Martínez of Taos, and with the kind assistance of Acting Chief Curator Vicente M. Martínez.

SANM = Spanish Archives of New Mexico (references are to the roll and frame number of the microfilm edition).

SRCA = State Records Center and Archives, Santa Fe, New Mexico.

For Further Reading

THERE IS NO SINGLE, well-grounded volume on the history of Taos in the era of Severino Martínez, but the notes in this book provide a guide to more specialized sources upon which any future study will depend.

For broad reading on New Mexico, Marc Simmons, *New Mexico: A History* (New York: W. W. Norton, 1977), remains the best introduction.

For New Mexico and its place in the Spanish and Mexican worlds, see David J. Weber, *The Spanish Frontier in North America* (New Haven: Yale University Press, 1992), and *The Mexican Frontier, 1821–1846: The American Southwest under Mexico* (Albuquerque: University of New Mexico Press, 1982).

Politics in don Severino's day is best explained in Marc Simmons, *Spanish Government in New Mexico* (Albuquerque: University of New Mexico Press,

1968). For trade and commerce, see Max L. Moorhead, *New Mexico's Royal Road: Trade and Travel on the Chihuahua Trail* (Norman: University of Oklahoma Press, 1954), and John O. Baxter, *Las Carneradas: Sheep Trade in New Mexico, 1700–1860* (Albuquerque: University of New Mexico Press, 1987). New Mexico society is laid bare in Ramón A. Gutiérrez, *When Jesus Came, the Corn Mothers Went Away: Marriage, Sexuality, and Power in New Mexico, 1500–1846* (Stanford: Stanford University Press, 1991), and vignettes of day-to-day life are described engagingly in Marc Simmons, *Coronado's Land: Essays on Daily Life in Colonial New Mexico* (Albuquerque: University of New Mexico Press, 1991). Until a more critical and probing scholar supplants his work, the architecture of don Severino's era is best understood in Bainbridge Bunting, *Taos Adobes: Spanish Colonial and Territorial Architecture of the Taos Valley* (Santa Fe: Fort Burgwin Research Center and Museum of New Mexico Press, 1964), and *Early Architecture in New Mexico* (Albuquerque: University of New Mexico Press, 1976). E. Boyd's *Popular Arts of Spanish New Mexico* (Santa Fe: Museum of New Mexico Press, 1974) offers an encyclopedic account of don Severino's material world.

For Taos itself, Blanche C. Grant's anecdotal *When Old Trails Were New: The Story of Taos* (New York: Press of the Pioneers, 1934) unfortunately remains unsurpassed. F. R. Bob Romero and Neil Poese, *A Brief History of Taos* (Taos: Kit Carson Historic Museums, 1992), contains a thumbnail sketch. John O. Baxter, *Spanish Irrigation in Taos Valley* (Santa Fe: New Mexico State Engineer Office, 1990), is a gem of a book, providing larger understandings than its title suggests. The story of Taos's most illustrious son of the nineteenth century is best told by Angélico Chávez, *But Time and Chance: The Story of Padre Martínez of Taos, 1793-1867* (Santa Fe: Sunstone Press, 1981), and the controversy that surrounds him is suggested in the essays in *Padre Martínez: New Perspectives from Taos* (Taos: Millicent Rogers Museum, 1988).

Index

Abiquiú, 5, 6, 7, 8, 18; route from, 18(map)
Abreú, Santiago, 51
Alcalde (chief town magistrate): definition, 50
Allande, Pedro María de, 36
Americans: in Taos, 63–65, 75, 77; trade with, 34, 35, 52, 57, 60
Anza, Juan Bautista de, 10
Apodaca Pass, 19
Archaeological investigations, 91
Archuleta, Antonio, 24
Armijo, Manuel, 75–76
Arroyo Hondo, 25–26, 71
Ayuntamiento (town council) of Taos, 43, 50, 53

Baca, Bartolomé, 50, 60

Barreiro, Antonio, 17, 55, 59
Beaubien, Charles, 65
Bent, Charles, 65, 73-74, 75, 76
Boyer, Jack K., 90, 91
Branch, Alexander, 65
Bunting, Bainbridge, 89, 90: *Taos Adobes*, 89

Camino del Medio, 24
Cañon, 20
Carson, Kit, 65, 77
Cather, Willa: Death Comes for the Archbishop, 77–78
Cerro de la Gallina, 73
Chacón, Fernando de, 10, 20, 34
Chávez, Fernando de, 20

Chimayó Rebellion (1837), 76
Community grants, 25, 26
Córdova, José Ignacio, 50
Courtyards (placitas), vi, 1
Couse, E. Irving, 4
Crops, 9, 24, 26, 72

Defense: building for, 1, 9
Diputación (territorial assembly), 49–51, 52, 53, 62-63
Don Fernando de Taos, 20, 21, 55, 71; Chapel of Guadalupe in, 21, 23, 54; intermarriage in, 65; on trade route, 58-59
Don Fernando de Taos grant, 20
Dyson, Jack, 90

Economy, 2, 9, 71; barter, 10, 33; cash, 33; production, 10. See *also* Farming; Ranching; Trade
Education, 8-9
Escudero, Manuel, 63
Españoles (Spaniards), 6
Extranjeros (foreigners), 55, 63, 64–65

Farming, 9, 25, 72: expansion of, 11, 26, 73
Food shortage, 43
Fowler, Jacob, 43
Franciscans, 19, 21, 23, 54

Gallegos y Lucero, Teodora, 87
Gananciales (assets in marriage), 70
García, Tomás, 92
Genízaros (Hispanicized Indians), 6, 9, 11, 27–28
Gijoso land grant, 24
Gonzales, Virginia, 89
Gordon-McCutchan, R.C., 3
Gregg, Josiah, 17, 84, 86
Guadalupe chapel (at Don Fernando), 21, 23, 54
Gutiérrez, Ramón A., 28

Hacienda: term, 1, 25; myth of self-sufficiency, 25. See also House
Herding, 27
Hernández, José Cayetano, 44
Hidalgo, Miguel, 53
Hispanic population: growth in, 10, 21
House (Martínez): furnishings, 86; growth of, 24, 83, 88; inheritors of, 87; later ownership/occupation, 79, 83, 88-90; layout, 1, 83-84, 85, 88; location, 1; renovation, 4, 89, 90-91
Household chores, 28
Housekeeper (María Dolores), 27, 70

Indians: hostilities, 2, 6, 7, 9, 19, 20, 23, 40, 42–43, 44, 51, 73, 75, 78; peace, 2, 10, 11; Pueblo Revolt, 19; as servants, 9, 73; trade with, 9, 10, 33-34; trading for, 38, 39
Iron implements, 44, 57–58, 86
Irrigation, 24, 73
Iturbide, Agustín de, 48, 49

Kearny, Stephen Watts, 76
Kit Carson Historic Museums, 1, 3, 4,
Kit Carson Memorial Foundation, 90, 91, 92

Labor, 27
La Lande, Baptiste (Juan Bautista Lalanda), 34
La Loma, 20
Lamar, Howard Roberts, 12
Lamy, Jean Baptiste, 77
Land (Martínez): 11, 25–26, 71, 73
Land ownership: issues, 52
Leach, Art, 92
Lee, Stephen Louis, 65
Livestock, 9, 11, 26, 27, 71, 72, 73
Lobato, José Antonio, 24
Lower Ranchitos, 1, 20
Lucero, José Ignacio (son-in-law), 72
Lucero, Juan Manuel (son-in-law), 72
Lucero, Pablo, 26, 43
Lucero, Pedro Antonio, 38
Luna, Rafael, 60, 62

Markets: external, 33; haciendas and, 25. See *also* Trade
Marriage: with Americans, 65; law of property in, 70
Martín, Joaquín, 24
Martín, José (father), 6, 10
Martín, Juan, 8
Martín, Juana, 25
Martín, María de la Luz, 45
Martín, María Gertrudis, 9, 27, 70
Martínez, Antonio José (brother), 6, 28
Martínez, Antonio José (son), 23, 39, 53, 72, 74; Bishop Lamy and, 77; children, 45, 54, 65, 77; criticism of, 65; education, 8, 23, 45–46; as executor of will, 70; marriage, 45–46; politics, 50–51, 52, 53–54, 61, 63, 65, 74–75, 76, 77, 78; property, 11, 25–26, 71, 73; as priest, 3, 45, 74, 78; schools and, 52, 75
Martínez, Fares Elías (great-grandson) and Julia, 89, 90
Martínez, José Manuel (son-in-law), 70, 72

Martínez, José María de Jesús (son), 23, 72, 74, 87
Martínez, José Santiago (son), 23, 72, 73, 74, 75, 77, 87
Martínez, Juana María (daughter), 23, 45, 70, 72
Martínez, Juan Pascual Bailon (son), 23, 70–71, 72, 73, 77, 87, 89; death, 79, 88; inheritance, 70–71, 87; judge, 23, 74; in military, 74, 75–76; politics, 72, 77, 78; records of, 4
Martínez, María del Carmel (wife), 1, 28; background, 2, 5–6; death, 3, 71; family, 6–7, 8, 23; marriage, 7
Martínez, María Estefana (daughter), 23, 72
Martínez, Pascual (son). *See* Martínez, Juan Pascual Bailon
Martínez, Santiago. *See* Martínez, José Santiago
Martínez, Severino: as alcalde, 26, 39, 48, 50, 59–60, 61–63, 65; birth, 6; childhood, 2, 9; death, 3, 24, 69; family, 5–6, 7–8, 9–10, 23; in jail, 36–37, 39; marriage, 7; name, 6, 24; in territorial assembly (*diputación*), 49–51, 52, 62–63. *See also* Will
Martínez, Virginia, 89
Martínez y Gallegos, Agapito, 89
Máynez, Alberto, 26, 39
Melgares, Facundo, 42, 43, 44, 48, 49
Mexico: independence, 2, 48–49, 50, 52–53; trade with, 2, 57–58; United States and, 76–77
Milford, Jerome and Anne, 90
Military: in New Mexico, 51, 73, 76, 77
Mill, reconstruction of, 92
Miller, Skip, 4
Minge, Ward Alan, 4, 70, 90
Mining, 11, 34
Missions, 54
Mule, dispute over, 36–39
Mule trains, 34

Narbona, Antonio, 50, 59, 62, 63
National Register of Historic Places, 90
North American residents, 58, 59

Oñate, Juan de, 5
O'Ryan, Desmond, 89
Ortiz, Antonio José, 20
Ortiz, Juan Felipe, 52, 69
Ortiz, Matîas, 37, 39

Partidarios (herders), 27
Pattie, James Ohio, 63
Peña, Juan de Dios, 36, 37, 39
Pereyro, José Benito, 37

Pike, Albert, 64, 86
Pioneers, 5–8
Placitas (courtyards), vi, 1
Plaza de la Capilla, 5, 6, 7, 11
Plaza de la Purísma, 20
Plaza de Nuestra Señora de los Dolores, 20
Plaza de San Francisco, 20
Plaza de San Francisco de Paula, 20
Plaza de Santa Gertrudis, 20
Plaza de Santa Rosa de La Capilla, 5, 6, 7, 8, 11
Plaza of Santa Rosa de Lima de Abiquiú, 6, 11
Plazas (villages), 5, 20–21; of Taos Valley, 22
Politics: local, 74; territorial assembly, 49–51, 52, 75, 77
Pratte, Sylvestre, 61
Prentis, Nobel, 92
Priests, 23; lack of, 21, 54
Production: per capita, 10
Pueblo Indians: Spanish and, 19
Pueblo Revolt (1680), 19
Puestos (villages), 5
Punche (kind of tobacco), 9

Racial attitudes, 63–65
Ranching, 9, 25, 71, 72; expansion of, 11, 73
Ranchitos, 24
Ranchitos de Abajo (Lower Ranchitos), 1, 20
Ranchos de Taos, 20, 65
Read, Leona, 89
Richardson, Anthony, 4
Río Abajo, 25
Río Arriba, 11, 25
Río del Pueblo, 1, 20
Río Fernando de Taos, 20
Rito Colorado: property at, 11, 71
Robidoux, François, 59–60, 61–62, 65
Romero, Luisa, 60
Rowland, John, 65

Sage, Rufus, 64
Salazar, Trinidad, 26
Sánchez, Antonio, 39
Sánchez, Francisco, 38
Sánchez, Miguel, 39
San Cristóbal: Martínez lands at, 26, 73
San Francisco del Ranchito, 24, 71
San Francisco de Paula, 20, 21
San Francisco de Paula del Ranchito, 24, 71
San Gerónimo de Taos church, 21, 23
Santa Anna, Antonio Lopez de, 74, 75
Santa Fe Trail, 58, 61

Santa Rosa: property at, 71
Santa Rosa de La Capilla, 5, 6, 7, 8, 11
Santisteban Coronel, Juan Antonio, 7
Santo Tomás de Abiquiú, 54
Sarracino, Rafael, 51
Schneider, Albert, 91
Schooling, 23, 52, 75
Serrano, Hernán and Luis Martín, 5
Servants, 9, 27–28, 70, 73
Shaeffer, Martin, 89
Sibley, George, 61
Smallpox, 7, 10, 23
Smuggling, 58, 60–61
Spanish Colonial architecture, 1, 90
Status (of the family), 8
Steele, Thomas, 78
Storrs, Angustus, 57, 58, 63

Tamarón, Pedro, 19
Taos, 3; ayuntamiento (town council), 43, 50, 53 Martínez move to, 11, 19, 24; mission at, 54
Taos Pueblo, 19; first Spanish contact, 19; Hispanics living in, 19; as parish headquarters, 54
Taos Rebellion (1847), 3, 76, 77
Taos Valley, 17, 19, 22
Territory (New Mexico as a), 49, 51, 77, 78; *diputacion* (territorial assembly), 49–51, 52, 53, 62–63
Tobacco, 9
Tourism, 2, 92

Trade, 33–36, 43, 71; with Americans, 34, 35, 52, 57, 60; with Indians, 9, 10, 33; items, 10, 11, 33–35, 57; with Mexico, 2, 57–58, 78; mule trains, 34; smuggling, 58, 60–61
Treaty of Guadalupe Hidalgo, 77
Trujillo, Francisca de la Luz, 7
Trujillo, Juana, 24
Trujillo, Vicente, 38

United States, 74; relations with, 44, 75–76, 77
Upper Ranchitos, 20

Valdés, José Martín and Micaela (parents), 6
Valdez, Santiago, 77
Vara (unit of length), 7
Vargas, Diego de, 7, 19
Vecinos (Spanish residents), 9, 10, 11, 19, 20, 33, 43
Vigil, Juan de Jesús, 39
Vigil y Alarid, Juan Bautista, 60, 61–63
Vocales (assemblymen), 49

Water, 24
Wealth, 23, 39
Will (of Severino Martínez), 3, 4, 91; estate, 26, 35–36, 45, 71; inheritors, 70–71, 87; instructions in, 69
Women, 3; assets in marriage (*gananciales*), 70; behavior, 64–65; education, 8-9;
Workman, William, 65